75

John W. Cox

March. 1955.

LIGHTHOUSES

LIGHTHOUSES

and Other Talks

to

Children and Young People

by

JOHN WILDING

LUTTERWORTH PRESS
LONDON

PRINTED IN GREAT BRITAIN BY
BRISTOL TYPESETTING COMPANY
STOKES CROFT   -   BRISTOL

PREFACE

I N offering this second volume of Talks for the use of my fellow-ministers and fellow-teachers I can only repeat what I said by way of preface to the first. It is not intended that anyone should read or recite these addresses as they stand. This is a book of material, mostly historical and biographical material. Anyone who takes any of it will want to shape it for himself, give it local and topical bearing and spice it with his own humour. I shall then count him no more in my debt than I am to the volumes of history and biography from which the incidents and illustrations have been taken. To one set of books I must, however, express particular indebtedness. The volumes of *The King's England,* edited by Arthur Mee, are rich mines which amply repay exploration.

J.W.

" I spoke to the children : the most difficult part of our office."

JOHN WESLEY.

" He had a singular dexterity to fill these narrow vessels with a funnel."

Said of LANCELOT ANDREWES.

" I take not any piece of true learning to be useless."

RICHARD BAXTER.

" I have never claimed to create anything out of nothing : I have always needed an incident or a character as a starting point."

SOMERSET MAUGHAM.

ACKNOWLEDGMENT

The quotations on pages 45 and 105 from the Moffat translation of the Bible are included by permission of Hodder and Stoughton Ltd., Warwick Square, London, E.C.4, who hold the copyright in this translation.

CONTENTS

CONTENTS

I

LIGHTHOUSES

THE old boys' books were so often wrong. Far too many of them left us with the idea that to be a hero a man had to be a soldier. That just isn't true. Stories of war may be thrilling, but they are stories of destruction. There are heroes of peace, and in the saving of lives great gallantry has been displayed.

We can take the story of the lighthouse as an example. The story opens in the centuries before Christ and it is by no means closed yet. Fully told it would take us round all the dangerous places round all the earth's coasts. It would introduce us to gallant souls like Henry Winstanley and Grace Darling, determined to save those in peril on the sea, and to villains like the wreckers deliberately destroying ships and men for the sake of plunder.

The story opens in Egypt where a lighthouse called the Pharos was built at Alexandria about 250 years before Christ. It was such a wonderful building that men called it one of the Seven Wonders of the World. It was constructed of marble blocks cemented together by molten lead, and it stood about 500 feet high. There for more than 1500 years its light shone out to guide sailors of all nations in and out of port. Storms left it unshaken, but an earthquake brought it down at last.

Four hundred years after it fell there were only seventy lighthouses in all the world. To-day there are nearly that many in and around New York Harbour alone. The story of how these life-saving lights have been planted on every coast, on dangerous reefs of rock and sand, is a story of heroic perseverance in the face of strange and terrible difficulties, to the overcoming of which men even gave their lives.

Here, for instance, is a long bank of sand far out from some shore. Ships could so easily run upon it. So it must be marked with a lighthouse. But how do you build a tower, tall enough to show its light for miles and sturdy enough to withstand winter's gales, on a foundation of loose sand? A solid foundation of concrete and steel must be laid before the great tower can be built.

Or, perhaps it is a low reef of rock that must be marked, barely appearing above the sea but capable of ripping the bottom out of a liner. How can you build with your feet in water? There are low rocks like that off the northern coasts of France which set the engineers a teasing problem. In two years the building gangs were only able to land twenty-two times, and in all they did twenty-six hours' work. It took fourteen years to build that lighthouse.

We all know something of the dogged perseverance which gave us the Eddystone. There off the south-west coast of England is a cruel ridge of rock around which the sea swirls and eddies. We do not know how many ships have struck upon it. Henry Winstanley made up his mind to build a tower there with a warning light. In 1699 the first Eddystone Lighthouse was completed. But in November 1703 it fell in a dreadful storm and Winstanley and five companions perished together. Men built a second and that was burned down. Then they built a third and that stood until it began to look unsafe and had to be taken down. When you stand to-day on Plymouth Hoe and look out across the breakwater you can see the fourth Eddystone fourteen miles away standing up like a thin pencil on the horizon.

What tales could be told of lighthouse keepers, living such lonely lives in the hottest and coldest places on earth, sometimes, even to-day, cut off for weeks at a time by raging storms.

Sometimes the light is not on a tower at all but on a ship over a shoal or even on a buoy filled with gas to keep the flame burning.

But what use is a light when it cannot be seen? None at all. So for time of fog we have lighthouses equipped with bells, whistles and sirens whose booming voice can be heard above any storm.

This war against peril at sea is so urgent that it has even brought warring nations together. When the English were busy on the Eddystone, French warships swooped down and carried off the workmen. When the French king, Louis XIV, heard of what had happened, he immediately ordered their return. " I am at war with England," he said, " not with humanity." It is good to hear such a saying. There is the hope for the future, that in war against their common dangers and difficulties men will forget their strife and unite to save. That is the hopeful lesson we may learn from the story of the lighthouse.

2

FOND OF BABIES

"A little child shall lead them." ISAIAH 11 : 6.

WHY are we all fond of babies? A minister will notice, when there is a christening, that when the baby is brought in all heads will turn that way : and afterwards one and another will ask if they may see the baby. It is very strange when you think what a nuisance babies can be. You would think that people would say, " Babies! Why, we've seen *and heard* enough of them! Take them away!" But no, we all love babies.

And so it has been for longer than we can tell. Here is a story which comes from long ago which proves that. The story was written down by an old Greek, a wonderful teller of tales called Herodotus. It shows that more than 2,300 years ago men, yes, even men, loved babies.

The story opens in Corinth, a famous Greek city, ruled at that time by a few, all members of one family. In this family was a daughter called Labda. Now when the time came for Labda to marry she went outside Corinth to Petra for her husband. Concerning the marriage a curious prophecy was made and whispered all about the city. It said that justice would come to Corinth, meaning the punishment of her harsh rulers, through a son of the marriage.

You can guess with what concern people waited to see if Labda would have a son. She did. The rulers of

Corinth then felt as King Herod felt when he heard that a new King of the Jews was born. They were afraid, and fear made them cruel. They determined to destroy the child before he should grow up to destroy them. So ten soldiers were found who bound themselves by an oath to kill him. Ten determined and cruel men against one innocent little baby! What earthly chance had the baby?

We had better follow the men on their vile errand. They made their way from Corinth to Petra. In Petra they sought out the palace of the Princess Labda. Here they told a carefully made-up story which brought out the Princess. Then they persuaded her to let them see her little son. Now, their plot was this. They would ask to hold the baby and the first man to take it in his arms would kill it by dashing it on the ground.

Not suspecting anything of this, Princess Labda brought out the baby in her arms and then in a fateful moment handed it to one of the ten soldiers. As he took it, something happened, something quite simple, something quite unforeseen, something which entirely upset the plan. "By a divine chance," as old Herodotus puts it, the baby smiled up into the face of the man who held out his arms for it. That did it! The baby smiled. The man was gripped with a sudden pity. He just could not kill a baby which smiled at him, and so, hastily, he handed it to the next man. What did he do? Hurl it to the ground? No! He, too, took one look at that happy, smiling face and handed it to the next man. And he? We can all guess how the story went on. One man passed the child to another, until at the end of this row of great, silly, soft men number ten gave the baby back unharmed to his mother. What they said among themselves as they shambled sheepishly away is something that we are not told. And, perhaps, that is a good thing! Nor do we learn what their brutal employers said when they returned to Corinth with the deed not done.

What we do learn is the wonderful truth of a simple saying in the Bible, " A little child shall lead them." It certainly led those men away from wickedness and cruelty to mercy and right. And I believe that God sends us these babies to keep our hearts tender and loving. Without them we might grow up so hard. With them He keeps our hearts more like His : for we know that He loves the little ones with all His heart.

One of the wisest and the best of Bishops long ago used some beautiful words, quaint words that young and old can learn and remember. He spoke of " the sweetening of the world by infants". That is a wonderful work which the very tiniest, without knowing it, can be used by God to do. God is busy in our hearts, sweetening them, when we are fond of babies.

3

THE SEPARATOR OF FIGHTING BULLS

" Blessed are the peacemakers." MATT. 5 : 9.

THERE were many people, even during his lifetime, who did not like Cecil Rhodes after whom Rhodesia is named. There still are many. He had his faults, but our story is about his virtues.

In the year 1896 a fierce revolt had broken out among the Matabele, the fighting descendants of the Zulus. It was said that 10,000 troops would be needed to put down the revolt, and those whose responsibility it was were very anxious. Rhodes said that he thought it was possible to stop the revolt without fighting. He declared that he was ready to go and meet the Matabele chiefs in the Matoppo Hills and there to talk peace with them. The Commander of the British Forces was opposed to any such a step. He feared that the chiefs would act treacherously, seizing Rhodes and killing him. But Rhodes persisted, and finally with three others he planned to meet the Matabele some four miles from the British camp.

Setting out on their horses, Rhodes and his little party drew near to the appointed spot. They were immediately surrounded by several hundred natives fully armed with guns and assegais—the deadly broad stabbing spear. Cecil Rhodes's chief companion, named Colenbranden, shouted out to his companions in alarm,

B

" Keep on your horses!" All did keep on their horses, except Rhodes. He leaped off, waved the yelling warriors aside and ran toward the chiefs. He began at once to rebuke them in the Matabele language for coming to an *indaba*, a parley or peace-talk, armed. He cried that he would have no further word with them while a single man had a gun in his hand.

In three minutes every gun was laid down. In three hours peace was made.

Cecil Rhodes's enemies always said that he lacked courage. Perhaps he did not care for fighting. But this was one of the bravest things ever done, unarmed to face such warriors in their passion and to demand and to win peace.

It is not surprising to learn that the Matabele so admired Rhodes for what he did that they gave him a special name among themselves. They called him " *Lamula 'Mkunzi.*" What does it mean? It means " The Separator of Fighting Bulls." What a picture that calls up, of two enraged monsters rushing upon each other, and of a man of such courage as to drive them apart.

A man like Rhodes is needed in Africa to-day. There white and black in some parts eye each other with hatred, hard things are said and done. Africa needs a man who can step between the two and bring peace between white and black. She needs a man who can show how both can live and work for the future of that wonderful country.

It is nearly fifty years since Rhodes died, but the work of the peacemaker has still to go on and still is blessed by God, the God and Father of white and black.

4

TRUTH WILL OUT

"Each man's work shall be made manifest: for the day shall declare it." 1 COR. 3 : 13.

SOME miles north of Oxford and at the very edge of the Cotswold Hills lies the village of Cropredy, a quiet enough place now, with fewer than five hundred inhabitants. Some three hundred years ago it was the scene of sharp fighting between the Cavaliers and the Roundheads. The fine Church tower, which visitors admire, stood and looked down on it all, for it was three hundred years old then.

If you go inside the Church, you will see its special treasure. The Bible from which the Lessons are read rests upon an old lectern, one of the fifty oldest in all England. It is made of brass. The big Bible rests on the stiff outspread wings of an eagle which is standing upon a globe. Now this lovely lectern was there in the Church when the Roundheads and Cavaliers were approaching. The people of Cropredy loved their Church and its treasures, and they thought that the desperate soldiers might damage them. So it was decided to hide those that could be moved. And where do you think they hid the brass lectern?

Very early one morning, while the mists still hung about the meadows, a few men stole out of the Church carrying it carefully between them. They made their way to the banks of the little River Cherwell and dropped the lectern in. You can be sure that they marked the place well so that when the dangerous days were passed their treasure might be recovered.

Years passed before they decided that it was safe to fetch it out. And it turned out to be harder than they thought. The heavy lectern had sunk into the mud and it was only after much fishing and splashing and straining that they got hold of it and dragged it out on to the bank. When it was cleaned and examined everyone was alarmed to find that there was one part missing, a piece from the stand at the bottom, one of three chubby little brass lions. You can guess what a hunt began. The people fished and prodded and raked and scooped in an effort to find the missing lion : but it has never been found from that day to this.

It seemed that there was only one thing to do and that was to make another. A craftsman said that he could make another all right. It would not be of brass, however, but of bronze : and he said that no one would be able to tell the difference. When the work was done and the lectern was back in its proper place, no one could tell the difference, at least not for a very long time. But now, after all these years and all the polishing it has had, the bronze shows up different from the brass, the false can be detected and told from the true. There are two bright little lions and there is one dark little lion and no one with an eye for detail can miss the difference.

I wonder if the people who go to Church there and listen to the Lessons being read from the lectern ever read the message of that little lion? You see, we are told in the Bible that if we put any sham into our work for God, it will one day be shown up. And there it is under our very noses! If there is anything in our work or our life that is only pretence, it will come out sooner or later. Only the best will do for God, both in His house and in His servants, only the true, the sincere.

That word "sincere" is an interesting one, by the way. Our one word "sin-cere" is really two Latin words meaning "without wax." It goes back to the bad ways of old sculptors. Chipping away, say, at a statue, they sometimes went a bit too deep or cracked off a bit that should have remained. What did they do? Scrap that piece and start again? No. They filled up the crack or made good the missing fragment with wax. It set hard and deceived the customer into thinking that he had a perfect piece of work—for a time. It *was* a perfect piece of sculpture that was "sin-cere," "without wax," just as perfect as it looked. And a sincere man or woman is sound, with no imitations, no pretences, but good all through and real in every way. If a day of temptation or trial comes to them, they are still as good as ever, still as loving, still as happy, still as upright. As the years go by they are still the same, the genuine article through and through, from beginning to end. These are the people who love and serve God with *all* their heart and mind and soul and strength. They can say at the end what General William Booth said, "He has had the whole of me."

5

GOD ENTRUSTS TO ALL

"Thou deliveredst unto me . . . talents."
MATT. 25 : 20.

Auda Abu Taya was an Arab sheik, or chief, of great fame. Many a story is told of his courage and noble spirit. Once he was leading a raid against an enemy tribe. As Auda and his men on their Arab steeds charged into the enemy camp a man surrendered to Auda, who in the name of Allah, the good and merciful, spared his life and promised that no harm should come to him. As Auda turned away to hasten on to battle, the prisoner begged for some token which he could show to the other raiders as proof that their chief had indeed promised him his life. Hastily, Auda pulled off the splendid handkerchief that was tied over his head, threw it to the man, and then rode off into the thick of the fight bareheaded.

Years passed, several years, and the incident had faded from Auda's mind completely. Then, one day, he received a message from one of the old enemy tribe saying that he was looking after a flock of goats for Auda. Auda knew nothing of any goats. However, in the end, the mystery was cleared up. It seems that the prisoner of the raid kept tight hold of Auda's kerchief and was eventually allowed to go free, still keeping the kerchief. Now the true desert Arab has a keen sense of honour. This man could not keep for himself what was not his

22

property. But with war between the tribes he could not return the kerchief. So what he had done was this. He sold Auda's kerchief and bought a goat. That goat prospered and grew into a flock. And so, although Auda had forgotten all about the kerchief and all about the man, the goats were there, they were his, and later he received them safely.

Jesus said we are all like men who have received loans from God, some great, some small. Some take all and keep all for themselves : others say, " I must use all for God. I must develop my talents." Like the captive tribesman they think that it would be theft just to use their God-given powers of sight, hearing, speech, powers of brain and hand, for themselves only. They do their best, and do all for God.

Let me tell you of a strange, great man who so used the gifts, the talents, with which God had entrusted him. He was a black man with a big name, George Washington Carver. He was born a slave, no one ever knew exactly when, and he never remembered his father or mother. When he was just a baby, he and his mother were stolen. The mother was sold away and the baby was brought back. His master gave the little black fellow some schooling. But one day he saw a terrible thing. He saw a fellow slave brutally killed by some white men. Horrified, George fled away. For ten years he wandered about, sweeping yards, sawing timber, harvesting. Somehow he managed to get more schooling. In 1890, at the age of 25, he went to College and the next year to the Iowa Agricultural Institute. Then in 1896 he moved to the Tuskegee Institute for Negroes and there he stayed for nearly fifty years, a whole lifetime of study and teaching. George Washington Carver saw that the Southern States of America were making a big mistake.

They were growing too much cotton. It was all right while crops were good and crops sold well. But when crops began to fail, then it meant utter disaster for all. So he experimented with other possible crops. First he tried peanuts. Now his work lay not just in showing that they could be grown, but in proving how useful they could be. He found 300 different things could be made from peanuts! There was a kind of flour, tapioca, vegetable milk, ice-cream powder, cattle and pig food, ink, cosmetics. Not satisfied with this, Dr. Carver next took the sweet potato and again he showed that it was possible to make many things out of it, syrup, flour, all kinds of meal, breakfast foods, tapioca and sauce. And these are only a few of the many products of the sweet potato.

So Carver gave new possibilities and new wealth to the South. What a clever man, you say. But he was more than that. He who had been so bitterly poor refused to make any profit out of his discoveries. He refused in words that we do well to remember: " God *gave* them to me, how can I *sell* them to someone else?" His talents came from God and all his work was done for God. He did not keep anything for himself but turned it all into riches for all God's family. So George Washington Carver died in 1942, a poor man who served the Southern States and set an example of the use of talents to all humanity.

6

GOD HEARS SHORT PRAYERS

"They think that they shall be heard for their much speaking. Be not . . . like unto them."

MATT. 6 : 7 and 8.

WHEN we are young, all of us, at some time or other, find the same difficulty. We can't think of anything to say in our prayers. " God bless Mother and Father," we say. " God bless me and make me a good boy, and . . . and . . ." And there it fades out. Yet left there it sounds so silly and short.

Of course, it is short : but that does not mean that it is silly. I once heard one of the most famous Christians alive prove that, without knowing what great comfort he was giving to many of his hearers. He is a Japanese, and his name is Kagawa. Of all the interesting and exciting things that he said to the meeting where I heard him speak, I remember one especially. He was telling us about the time when he was turning toward our Christian religion. He had learned about the loving Father-God, and he knew that he must seek His help. So young Kagawa began to pray. He used to pray at night when he went to bed, and because he knew he would be persecuted for becoming a Christian, he used to pray secretly. " I pulled the bedclothes up over my head," he said to us, " and prayed hard." Now it must have been a wonderful prayer to have had such a wonderful answer so that he became such a wonderful man. What was the prayer? He told us. " God make me a good boy. O God, make me a good boy." The prayer that helped to make Kagawa a Christian saint may have been short and so like ours. But it cannot have been silly. And it must have been heard.

Don't worry if your prayers are short. It is not how long they are that matters. What matters is how deeply and really you mean them. You see, you can mean a lot in a few words, if they are words from your very heart.

There is a good story from old France to show that. It comes from a time when the real ruler in France was the Cardinal Mazarin. Being a great power in the land he was overwhelmed with people begging him for favours. One day the Governor of the Bastille, that Paris prison and fortress, begged the Cardinal to see a relative of his who wished to ask a favour. At first the Cardinal refused, saying that he had no time. " But," said the Governor, " he only wants a minute of your time and just to say two words." " All right," replied the Cardinal, " I will hear him : but, remember, he is only to say *two words*."

The Governor had not meant it just like that and he went off a bit bewildered. His relative, however, was not worried. Two words would be enough. When he went to see Cardinal Mazarin it was a very cold day. So, as he entered the room, the petitioner looked toward the blazing fire, shivered, and said, " Cold !" Then he rubbed his hands over his stomach and said, " Hungry !"

Mazarin laughed. Two words the man was to say : and two only he had said. So Mazarin very wittily gave the two-word petition a two-word answer. Calling out, " Fire ! Bread !" he wrote out an order for a pension to be granted.

GOD HEARS SHORT PRAYERS

Few words from the heart mean more than many words slipping easily off the tongue. On November 19, 1863, there were spoken the most famous words in American history. The terrible Civil War had been raging for over two years, a battle had been fought in the July of that year at Gettysburg and it was decided to set apart a portion of the very battlefield as a national cemetery for the fallen. Two men were to speak at the ceremony. Edward Everett spoke first, for two hours. Abraham Lincoln then spoke for two minutes. What Everett said, no one has cared or remembered. Lincoln's few words will never be forgotten.

It is no wonder that Jesus said that men are not heard for their " much speaking." He must have heard of how the heathen would beseech some idol, crying out to it hour after hour. " They think that they shall be heard for their much speaking. Be not . . . like unto them." We are not to be like them because God is not like that. He will hear any sincere prayer, be it only a word. So Jesus told his people to say short, real prayers, and as an example He gave to them the prayer which all His people use, the Lord's Prayer.

Jesus loved real prayers. Do not worry if your prayers are short. Real prayers can be, most often are, short. But God hears them all.

7

THE GOLDEN WHEAT-EAR

For fifty-one Sundays in the year, in our Churches, the flowers have it all to themselves. To-day, on Harvest Sunday alone, other things get a look in, fruit, vegetables and corn. Flowers, of course, are important. We all like them and look for them. But you cannot eat flowers. You would sooner have cabbage than roses for dinner to-day, wouldn't you? I would sooner have carrots than carnations.

So, without despising the flowers, we must ask them to step back a bit to-day and to let the other important things have their one day, at least, in the place of honour. And, perhaps, at Harvest Festival we are right to give first place of all to the corn. If you say the word " harvest " to most people in England, they think first of corn, and I'm sure they are right. What Shakespeare called " our sustaining corn " ought to have the place of honour.

Let me tell you how a king was once convinced of that. He was Henri IV of France. He happened once to be staying at the palace of Fontainebleau. As the King was walking through the famous gardens, he noticed a humble fellow standing on the terrace and gazing at all the beauties of the flower-beds.

" What are you looking at, my good man?" asked the King.

" At your gardens, Sire, for they are very fine," replied the man. "But," he added, " I have a garden which is far better."

" Where is your garden?" enquired the King.

" At Malesherbes, Sire," was the answer.

" Well," said the King, " I should very much like to see it. What is your name?"

" My name is Lefoy, and I am your Majesty's humble servant."

Some time later, it happened that the King was driving in the direction where Lefoy lived, so he turned aside and asked to be shown Lefoy's garden. Then the man was found, and he led the King to a huge cornfield in splendid condition. The King gazed at it for a moment, and then he turned to Lefoy and said, " You are right. This garden is finer and better than mine." And to prove how much he valued the man's good farming and to encourage others in the same work, the King granted Lefoy the privilege of wearing a golden wheatear in his cap.

The old Chinese are said to have had a proverb, " If you have two loaves, sell one and buy a lily." Man needs beauty as well as bread. But during the war many people had to turn the proverb round! They dug up flower gardens to grow food. We learned during that war not to take necessary things for granted.

We said, " Give us this day our daily bread," with a new thoughtfulness. Don't let us lose that. Let this day remind us all again of what God gives in all the treasures of the earth that we may be fed and strong to learn and work.

8

AN ARCHBISHOP'S BAD MANNERS

"In honour preferring one another." ROM. 12 : 10.

THE first wave of Christianity came to Roman Britain and spread slowly. Then came the frightful storm of the Saxon invasion on our east coast, driving the Christians before it into the far west of Wales and Cornwall. Those heathen Saxons settled down and the country grew peaceful. At length came the second wave of Christianity led by Augustine sent from Rome. He knew, of course, of the old Christians away there in Wales and Cornwall and he tried to join up with them. So he sent a message asking them to meet him in Gloucestershire, and seven bishops and several learned men agreed to come.

These Christians of Wales and Cornwall had lived apart for so long that they were suspicious of Augustine and the great Church of Rome which he represented. He might want to become their overlord and to change their ways. So before they went to the place of meeting, they consulted a wise hermit about what they should do.

" If Augustine be a man of God," he answered, " follow him."

" Yes," they said, " but how shall we know that he is a man of God?"

Then the hermit made this reply. " Our Lord said, ' Take my yoke upon you, and learn of me; for I am meek and lowly in heart '. If this Augustine is meek and lowly of heart, then it is the yoke of Christ that he wears and the yoke of Christ that he offers unto you. If, however, he is stern and haughty, he is not of God and you are not to listen to him."

" Yes," said the bishops, " but how are we to know that he is meek and lowly of heart?"

Then the hermit made this suggestion. " Arrive at the place of meeting *after* Augustine. He will then be seated. If he rises from his chair to give you welcome, listen to him. But if he remains seated, then it will be plain that he despises and will humble you."

The hermit's advice was taken. When they knew that Augustine had arrived at the place of meeting, the bishops and learned men of Cornwall and Wales drew near.

Augustine saw them coming. He remained seated.

The bishops protested at his discourtesy, accused him of pride and refused to listen to his proposals.

That is how the bad manners of an Archbishop hindered the work of God. Instead of the scattered parts of the Church coming together to face wickedness and idolatry, they remained separated for many more years.

People do make up their minds whether we are worth listening to by what we show ourselves to be. They hear us speak unkindly or see us treat each other rudely or harshly. Then, they cannot hear any talk of love and grace. If they do, it isn't convincing. It is, as we say, " pure talk " and no more. And it is not just our talk but our lives that will make this world a better, a more Christian place.

9

WRITTEN BUT NOT POSTED

" Be ye angry, and sin not." EPH. 4 : 26.

WHEN a letter has been written, what happens to it?
It is put into an envelope and then it is put into
a pillar-box. Always? It depends on the sort of letter
you have written. There was once a great man who was
not at all sure that that was where *all* letters ought to go.

He was Abraham Lincoln, the famous President of
the U.S.A. During the terrible Civil War Edwin M.
Stanton, the Secretary for War, came to Lincoln in a
great rage. It seemed that Stanton was wild with an
officer who had failed to obey orders.

" I believe I'll sit down," he cried, " and give him a
piece of my mind."

" Yes, do," said Lincoln. " Sit down and write it now,
while it is on your mind. Make it sharp! Cut him up!"

Hastily Stanton drew up a chair. His pen fairly flew
across the sheets as he told the officer exactly what he
thought of him. He was so pleased with the result that
he read it over to Lincoln.

" That's right," said Lincoln. " That's a fine letter."

" Now I wonder," said Stanton half to himself, " I
wonder how I can get it to him? Who shall I get to
take it? Ah, I think I'll send it . . ."

" Send it?" said Lincoln who suddenly caught what
Stanton was saying. " *Send it?* Why, don't send it. Tear

32

it up. You've got all that off your mind. That's all that was necessary. Now tear it up. You should never want to *send* such letters. I never do."

Abraham Lincoln was not the only man who thought in that way. There was an Archbishop of Canterbury who died nearly sixty years ago whose name was Edward Benson. A fine-looking man, they said that his character was as beautiful as his face. When his son went to the Archbishop's desk after his death, he found one drawer labelled " Letters." Inside that drawer was a notice pasted on to the wood. It said,

Rule   Not to answer for 24 hours any letters which
        on any account make my heart beat faster.

He knew that some letters he received would deeply disturb him. If he wrote back at once, he might write with anger or resentment. Such letters ought not to be written, or being written ought not to be sent.

We cannot help feeling cross about some things. We ought to feel cross when we see good work hindered by idleness, meanness or selfishness. But we ought not to write or say or do hasty or unkind things. We should wait until we are sure that love has had its say as well as anger. Then the sharp things will not be said. They will die on our lips. Then the letters may be written, but they will not be posted.

St. Paul put the message in a sentence, " Be ye angry, and sin not ". You may feel, but you must not be carried away by feeling.

Good, wise St. Paul! Good, wise Abraham Lincoln! Good, wise Archbishop Benson! Good and wise you and I, if we truly take their counsel to heart and remember to act on it all our days.

C

10

OLD GRANDMOTHER

THAT wasn't a very polite name to give to a woman —" Old Grandmother ". Perhaps if we had seen her in her old-fashioned clothes, a long dark skirt reaching to the ground, a waistbelt, a long-sleeved white blouse, a high stiff collar with a tie, a sailor hat with a veil, and, of course, gloves, we might have thought that it was not so unsuitable a name after all. It was the name that the Blackfellows, the Aborigines of Australia, gave to Mrs. Daisy Bates—" Kabbarli," Old Grandmother. Never mind the name! She was one of the bravest, gentlest, most modest and most generous women who has ever lived.

Fifty years ago Australia was inhabited by a few million white people, newcomers to the continent, all round the coasts. Inland there roamed tribes of the most primitive blacks, perhaps 60,000 of them, whose ancestors had lived in Australia from the dimmest past. Facing the advance of a new and powerful civilization, the blacks lost heart and began to die out rapidly. Daisy Bates came to love and shield them in their passing. They knew that their day was done. " When I finish, all finish!" cried one. " I realized that they were passing from us," wrote Mrs. Bates. " I must make their passing easier."

Picture then this woman in her old-fashioned dress by wells and creeks and camps, on horse and on foot, collecting scraps of the language, old customs, legends, and all the time winning her way into the confidence of a shy people.

Where Kabbarli pitched her tent, there the aborigines came, and on them she lavished her care. She was their nurse in illness; measles, consumption, blindness, madness. Nothing frightened her and nothing disgusted her. She was too sorry for them to pity herself. And lest we should think of her life as a martyrdom, she pauses to tell of its joys as well as its hardships. She loved the country, every rock, bush and living thing, the sunrise and the sunset, the camp-fire.

I spoke of her generosity. She coolly records it thus: " At about this time I sold my pastoral properties . . . and so could provide liberal flour, sugar and tea for the forthcoming celebrations." These were native ceremonies to which many groups gathered, often hostile groups, and Kabbarli had the dangerous task of keeping the peace. Once she found them milling round in an armed mob. She pushed her way in. " All you grandsons, bring your spears here to me," she said quietly. " I will sit down and take care of them and then you can go a little way and have a good fight and come back for food." Off they went, made a glorious row, and then came back for the meal she provided!

I spoke of Mrs. Bates's care for the blind. She once found three blind and helpless natives just deserted by their own folk. So she pitched her tent where she found them and because they needed her she stayed and cared for them for two or three years. One of these blind folk was a cannibal, a murderer many times over, blinded by lightning and half-mad. Him she tended till he died, digging his grave and burying him with her own hands.

It was to this same camp that another waif came to

die, a woman. As she began to sink she caught Kabbarli's hand in hers. " Where am I going?" she cried in fear. Mrs. Bates only met that question with another, " Is Kabbarli good?" " Kabbarli *is* good," she cried. " Then," said Mrs. Bates, " my Father is sitting down where you are going, and as soon as I let go of your hand, my Father will catch hold of it. He will take care of you till I come." " Your Father, Kabbarli? Then I shall be safe." And very peacefully that simple black woman fell asleep.

In this life, so simple and so hard, time seemed to have no meaning. Eight years were spent in one place, two in another, and three elsewhere. Then came the longest stay of all, sixteen years. To this camp floated remnants of dying groups. They were bitter enemies of each other yet they kept the peace in the shadow of Kabbarli. She in turn devoted to them her all. She received no help from the Government of Australia. She sold her last, cherished possessions, and in the end was depending entirely on what she could earn by writing about the aborigines.

Leave them? Whatever happened she could not think of that yet. " It was impossible to leave these people, to be deaf to their appeal for human kindliness . . . Somehow they became my responsibility." Her strength and her resources came near to their end in what she calls " years of increasing difficulty and disheartenment." When she was over seventy years of age Mrs. Bates was still leading this life.

Then came a brightening. In 1933 Mrs. Bates was called into consultation by the Government of Australia. In the New Year Honours List of 1934 she was made a Commander of the Order of the British Empire. Very simply she wrote, " This recognition from our beloved

Sovereign, coming as it did when my little camp was almost empty of provender and my heart of hope, has been the full reward of my life's service." As the years passed Mrs. Bates had made notes of all the things she had learned and seen of the aborigines, a colossal collection of unique knowledge of the thoughts and ways of a dying race. At last came the opportunity to return to civilization and to write about the history, the life, the mind and the soul of the aborigine. So at the age of 75, on Silver Jubilee Day, May 1935, Kabbarli turned back.

Her old clothes she gave to her friends who so proudly carried her boxes to the railway. They left her sitting on her luggage on the platform. There she recited to herself, " Now the day is over."

Looking back on it all Mrs. Daisy Bates said, " There was not an hour of my time wasted in all those years . . If the slightest impression of anything I have said or done, by example or in devotion, remains with them in comfort for the past or hope for the future, I shall be content."

It is not only with the aborigine that her example will remain. It is full of challenge and inspiration for all who hear her story.

II

WHERE ARE YOU GOING?

"I press toward the mark." PHILIPP. 3 : 14.

HE must have been a queer boy! He was born one hundred and fifty years ago, in France, near Bordeaux. When he and his playmates at school started boasting, as boys will, about what they were going to be and do when they grew up to be men, René Caillié said, "I'm going to go to Timbuktu."

Is there such a place? Oh, yes. For a thousand years men had told stories of a famous "lost" city away in the great Sahara Desert in North Africa. But no one had ever been there, so some scoffed at the idea. They said that there was no such place and when they wanted to be really rude to some one they said, "Go to Timbuktu!" That is how the word came to be such a joke. But some went on believing and tried to find Timbuktu. They believed that it was a rich place, rich in gold and rich with trade.

Then this boy René Caillié heard of this mysterious city. It fired his imagination and his ambition. He made up his mind that he would reach it, however long or however hard the journey. That in itself was not very strange, for boys do have wonderful dreams and promise themselves that they will do wonderful feats when they are grown up. Some of them could, if only they had the grit. Poor René hadn't a chance. You see, his father died in prison, and his mother was left with six little ones to feed and clothe. She died when René was only nine years old, so the little chap was sent off to his grandmother's. That would not have been so bad but for the fact that his grandmother, too, was desperately poor, and René had to leave school and go to work at a cobbler's. He stayed and worked with the cobbler until he was sixteen, and all the time he was dreaming of Africa and his heart was set on seeing Timbuktu. At the age of sixteen with 16 francs in his pocket (about £1, I think) he set out for Africa, for Timbuktu. It took him twelve years to get there. Yes, he got there in the end, but what a story and what a journey it was!

This youth of sixteen worked his way to Africa as an officer's servant at 18 francs a month. Within twenty-three days he was in Africa and it looked as though he would soon be in Timbuktu. I think he began to wonder why it had taken other people so long. Well, he soon found out. He fell ill. The climate and the food were strange. He could not seem to make any progress and he had to leave Africa, and it was two long years before he returned. This time he landed with only the clothes he stood up in. " Nothing," he said later, " nothing discouraged me." It was no idle boast.

He managed to join an expedition that was going out into the Sahara Desert and for four months he was able to study the land and learn about its people and their ways. He returned to Senegal and worked for some time as a cook. Then he obtained a post in an office. And all the time he dreamed of Timbuktu. He even had to carry his dreams back to France for a year or two, but in 1824 he was back in Africa once more.

By now, with all his knowledge and experience of Africa, René had made his plan for getting to Timbuktu.

The first part of the plan was to disguise himself as a Mohammedan. To learn how to do this really well, he lived with the Moors. He learned their ways and living their life he grew tough and hard and strong.

He saved money and at last he had 2,000 francs. Then he put the second part of his plan into operation. He became a merchant. He bought trade goods, paper, tobacco, glassware, handkerchiefs, knives and mirrors. Disguised as an Egyptian and pretending to be a Mohammedan, on April 19, 1827, he set out in quest of Timbuktu. It took him exactly a year and a day to find it. On April 20, 1828, he entered the city of his dreams. All he found when he reached it you must read elsewhere.

He stayed in Timbuktu for fifteen days, and by September 1828 he was safely on his way back to France. There he received a great prize for his discovery. He dined with the King, and he received both fame and fortune.

There are two things about René Caillié that strike me. He knew where he was going and he let nothing stop him from getting there. What he decided to do as a boy, he went on and did as a man. Neither poverty, illness nor peril could prevent him from reaching his goal.

There are days that come when we set out on a new stage of our life's journey. Do we know where we are going? Have we any goal? Some people have and some have not. Some drift on, taking trouble only to choose the easiest path through life. They are like the tramp with whom Lady Oxford once sheltered from the rain. She asked him about his life and how he decided where to go. " When you wake up in the morning," she asked, " how do you shape your course?" To which he answered, " I always turn my back to the wind." That is not the way in which great and useful lives are directed.

We look into the Bible and there we read of one of the greatest of all Christ's servants, St. Paul. He took the Good News of Jesus Christ to men of many races, in scores of cities, in two continents. He stood before Governors and Kings. He wrote books that will live and be loved for ever. Why was he able to be so splendid and do so much? The secret lies in five simple words, " I press toward the mark ". He was like a runner with his eyes on the tape. He had made up his mind and he just lived to know his Master, Jesus Christ, better, and to serve Him more faithfully every day.

When you think of it, that might be our aim, to live to know our Master better and to serve Him more faithfully every day. Let us bring to that aim the splendid determination we have heard of and seen in others. Let us bring all the courage and grit we have and like St. Paul give even more to finding the secret of a rich life than René Caillié gave to finding a rich city.

12

A KING'S WEDDING-RING

IN the very same year as the great men of England forced our bad King John to sign *Magna Carta*, 1215, a boy was born in France who was to be one of its noblest kings. He was called Louis and was the ninth of that name.

At his coronation service he showed the spirit in which he came to the throne. It was not a spirit of pride or joy in his great power. Very sincerely he uttered a prayer, " Good Lord, I lift up my soul unto Thee. I trust in Thee." He accepted the Kingship as a trust from God. There was a work for him to do for the welfare of his subjects and it could only be done with God's help. We know that King Louis IX sought that help in the Bible. We are told that he so loved his Bible that he caused candles to be made three feet long and sat reading while they lasted !

In the year 1244 he fell desperately ill and came near to death. While he was so ill he did what men often did then. He solemnly promised before God that if he recovered he would join a Crusade and go out to fight for the Holy Land. He did recover and kept his vow. In fact he went on two Crusades.

A large history book says that King Louis " kept two grand objects before his eyes, personal holiness and the happiness of his subjects." It is not surprising that admiration and love of a King so good and noble grew during his life, and that since his death he has been known as St. Louis.

Now this King had a secret which, I believe, explains his whole life. He carried about with him a pledge which no one could see. On one finger he wore a wedding-ring, and on that ring there were inscribed three words:

GOD   FRANCE   MARGARET

The ring was a pledge of his loyalty to all three of the great loves of his life, his God, his country, and his wife.

GOD. He began there. He was taught from childhood that God had given him life. Therefore he owed all love and obedience to God. You remember the first four words of the Bible, " In the beginning, God . . ." God first. If only men gave Him that first place, they would be better and life would be happier. It is true of kings and statesmen : it is true of the humblest and the youngest. Things get into a mess in our games and our homes and our countries because too many are really crying out like little children, " Me first !" When we make that our aim, then we start struggling one against another and the quarrels of a family grow into the wars of the world. Across the years we see an example, a life which put God first, and we know that that is right and we are wrong.

FRANCE. That came next. God had set Louis in a great country, and he was to love and serve that country with all his powers.

" God first," we said. Louis was not going to make the mistake which our own Wolsey made later. He grew to be a great man in the nation in the days of Henry VIII. While Henry was still a wild young man, the country at home and abroad was wonderfully served by Wolsey. But when he was old and dying he said the saddest of words, " If I had served God as I have served the King, He would not have given me over in my grey hairs." Wolsey put the affairs of kingdom first and forsook the service of his God. Louis put God first, and because of that he ever remembered his duty toward his people.

When in this country we have a son in the Royal Family, he is made Prince of Wales. His motto consists of two German words, *Ich Dien*, I serve. As Prince, and later as King, that is to be the spirit of his life, to serve his country. Every time Louis glanced at the ring on his hand he was reminded of that.

MARGARET. God had given to Louis a precious wife. He did not think of her as someone whom he had cleverly caught with his wit or his wealth. She was not, as often in those hard old days, someone made to marry him. She was God's gift. In marrying her, he took her at God's hand, and he promised God to love and cherish her all his life. Homes begun in that spirit are happy homes and all in them are secure.

I like to think of a King who was a Saint. I like to think of his three loyalties, so simple and so grand,

GOD   FRANCE   MARGARET.

13

THE CANDLE AUCTION

"Making the very most of your time."
EPH. 5 : 16 (Moffatt).

Have you ever been to an auction sale? If you have, you know how exciting it can be. You all know what happens. Suppose that it is a furniture sale. The auctioneer will describe an article and praise it while the possible buyers draw close. Then comes the question, "What am I bid for this handsome table?" Now suppose that you want it very badly. It may be a valuable piece of furniture worth £10. You hope to get it for £5. What do you do? You can start bidding at once, perhaps something low, say £1, to see if there is anyone else obviously keen to bid against you. If there is, the price will soon go up and up, £1, £2, £3, £4, up to £7 or £8 and you begin to wonder whether you had better give up. The other thing you could do would be not to bid at all to begin with. Let others do the struggling, and if the price does not go too high, swoop in at the end and carry off the prize. "Going," cries the auctioneer : and if you want to bid again you must be very quick, because he raises his little hammer and cries, "Going at £4. 10. 0. Going, Going . . . *Gone*." His hammer gives a rap on his desk and the last bidder wins. Once the hammer has fallen no more can be done.

I have read of a curious way of holding an auction

45

which was sometimes followed for a change. When the
sale was due to commence a new candle was brought in
and placed before the auctioneer. A ruler was then taken
and exactly one inch was measured from the top down
the candle and a pin was stuck firmly into it at that
point. The candle was lighted and began slowly and
steadily to burn down. Immediately it was lighted bidding could begin. Bidding was allowed to go on so long
as the pin remained in the candle. The article being
sold went to the maker of the last bid before the pin
dropped. A candle auction, as they called it, must have
been an amusing sort of affair. To have only so long and
to have to get in before the pin dropped must have been
really a strain, and I can imagine the laughing and the
cheering at the end.

A candle lighted and slowly and steadily burning
down is not a bad picture of the year before us. Even as
I speak it is going. And there is so much we want to get
into the year! It is as bad as the auction. We have to
get it in before the candle burns down! Oh, but a year
is a long time, you say. You think there is plenty of time
for all you want to do. Jesus knew people who said that.
He told a story about them. He said that there were ten
of these women going to an Eastern wedding. Now that
was very different from ours. The weddings that Jesus
knew were arranged like this. The bride went to the new
home with just her attendants, and was beautifully
dressed all ready to meet the bridegroom. He, meanwhile,
was some distance away at the house of a friend with
his attendants. When evening came the bridegroom
would call his friends to come with him and set out with
lanterns and torches to the new home where his bride
was waiting. Now, the ten women of whom Jesus spoke
were waiting with the bride to greet the bridegroom.

While they waited in the cool of the evening they all fell asleep. Suddenly came a thrilling cry: " The bridegroom is coming! Come and meet him!" They all jumped up to light their lamps. Five had seen to it that they had plenty of oil before they lay down to rest. Five had said to themselves that there would be plenty of time to see to that. And now the five foolish ones were caught. While they ran off to get oil the bridegroom came. They missed the procession: and when they got back they were all told they were too late for the feast.

There isn't plenty of time. The candle is burning down! St. Paul knew this. That is why he wrote to his friends at Ephesus, " Make the very most of your time!" He was so sure that that was the wise thing to do that he said it to his friends at Colossae as well, " Make the very most of your time!"

I have never forgotten some words I first met a long time ago which tell us how to do that. They would make a splendid New Year's resolution. " I shall pass this way but once; any good thing therefore that I can do or any kindness that I can show any human being, let me do it now, let me not defer it or neglect it, for I shall not pass along this way again." To keep that resolution would be to make the very most of our time and to make the New Year truly Happy.

14

WHAT CAN YOU SEE?

WHEN the good Victoria had been Queen of England
for sixty years, they had a wonderful celebration
in London. There was one of those glorious processions
which thousands and thousands of people gathered to
see. At the end of the long drive the old Queen said
rather drily, " I suppose that it was a very fine procession, but I wasn't in the best position for seeing it!"

What you see does depend on where you are. If you
came to me and said that you had drawn a picture and
called it " Morning Service," I should be very interested
to see it. It would probably show pews and the backs of
people in front of you, the Choir and the Table, the
pulpit, the minister and the organ. It would show the
things that you see week by week from where you sit.
But, suppose that I drew a picture of Morning Service?
There would be pews, with the children in front and the
people behind, all facing me. There would be the back
of the church and the entrance doors, and the clock
placed so cunningly that only the minister can see it.
Every Sunday the minister sees something very different
from you because he stands in such a different place.

I am reminded of the old man, a veteran of the wars
against Napoleon, who at a great age was taken to see
a picture by a famous woman artist, Lady Butler. It was
a picture of the Battle of Quatre Bras in which the old
man had fought, and he so much wanted to see it. At

last, he stood in front of it. A puzzled look came over his
face, a look of disappointment, and this is what he said :

> Well, it didn't look like that to me. You see, the lady
> that painted that picture was looking on at the square
> from the outside where she could see the faces of our
> men. I was inside where we couldn't see our own faces,
> but only the Frenchmen that were coming at us. No,
> Sir, it didn't look like that to me.

I always think of that when I hear people talking
about our Churches. They describe them in this way or
in that, and all the time what they see and what they
say depends on where they stand, inside or outside.
Sometimes when I listen to such people I want to say,
" No, Sir, it doesn't look like that to me ! "

I could write a description of a family, giving the
names and ages of Father and Mother and the children.
I could say what Father did for a living and whether he
liked gardening. I could find out where Mother went
shopping and whether she could cook a Christmas dinner. I could even find out what sort of reports the children had from school last term. But, if I went on telling
things like that for an hour, it would not tell us what
matters, what the spirit of the home is like, whether it
is good to live there, whether they love each other and
have fun together. I could only know that by living with
them in the home, and for some time.

So anyone can describe a Church from the outside,
telling how many people belong to it, how many children are in the Sunday School, what hymn-book we
use and how much money we raise. But, that does not
tell you the things that matter, the things that we who
are inside know. I mean, what joy it is to belong here,
how proud and glad we are to be coming here on Sun-

D

days, how good it feels to stand up together to sing the opening hymn on Sunday morning, how solemn it is to bow together to pray, how cheering in the week to meet someone else who belongs and to say, "See you down at Church to-night!"

To any who are still outside this must be said, "You will never know what the Church of Jesus Christ is really like until you come inside. What we tell you about it, we know to be true. Come in, and you will soon see and learn for yourselves what you can never see nor learn so long as you stay outside."

15

RELEASING THE FRAGRANCE

AT the end of a hot and dusty day we often get a cool
and quiet evening. What is the pleasantest thing to
do then? It is a grand time for a swim or for a row on
the river. It is just the time to get up on to the hills and
to look across the wide fields and woods. But, there is
one simple thing that I enjoy best of all. It is to walk
round a garden, if possible an old garden surrounded by
walls and with grass paths, all neatly kept.

You see how the peas and potatoes are getting on, the
strawberries and the currants. As you wander on there
is something which you are bound to find in these old
gardens, a corner devoted to herbs. There is a bed of
mint, a bush of sage, a root of thyme, marjoram, borage,
rosemary. What wonderful old names they are! What
delicious scents! I wonder if you could tell one from
the other? If we were to blindfold you and to put each
under your nose in turn, could you name it?

Now, a strange thing about these herbs is this. If you
just stand by and look at them, you notice no scent at
all. But if, as you pass by, you brush hard against them
or tread on a spray or break a bit off and crush it between your fingers, then the sweet scent is set free.

So it is with some people. You cannot guess how
splendid a spirit they have if you only know them in the
easy, ordinary day. To see them at their best, you must
see them in trouble, when they are hard pressed. Their

very best only comes out then. I think of George Washington who led the Americans in their War of Independence against Great Britain nearly 200 years ago. In that war Washington and his men at one time suffered terribly. They were twice defeated. The men were in such want that they marched barefooted through the snow and left it stained with their blood. A lesser man would have given up in despair. Yet Washington was never so great as in that awful winter in Valley Forge. " When the days were blackest men clung to his unfaltering courage as to the last firm ground in a rising flood." Or, I think of that splendid doctor, Edward Wilson, who went out with Scott's last expedition to the South Pole, and who died with him on the way back. Men found him cheerful, patient and encouraging in the long dark and fearful cold of the polar winter. " There is always something so reassuring about Bill," wrote his friend, " he comes out best in adversity."

That reminds me of one of the most lovable characters that Charles Dickens ever drew, Mark Tapley, in *Martin Chuzzlewit*. As soon as we meet him he begins to grumble—because his life is too easy! He is sure that his best will come out in a life that would make other men miserable. And in the story we see it happen, with the result that everybody loves Mark Tapley in the book. And, believe me, everybody loves Mark Tapley when they meet him, or her, in real life. It means to be brave in danger, hopeful in trouble, forgiving when hurt. That is to let our light shine so that men see that we have been with Jesus. This I should call the fine mark of a Christian, that he comes out best when things are worst, that under the rubs of life his spirit yields its sweetest fragrance. That is to follow Jesus. The closer He came to the cross, the more deep and tender His love, the more staunch His faith. Never does His strength and graciousness show more clearly than on the cross itself. It is there, when wickedness does its worst, that He cries, " Father, forgive them, for they know not what they do." It is there, in His own pain, that He most wonderfully comforts another, " To-day shalt thou be with me in Paradise."

It is that spirit of the Master that is to live in the disciple. When the way is hard, Jesus looks all the more eagerly for His spirit to shine forth in us. When it is hard, that is our great opportunity to give of His best and so to sweeten the world.

16

HE DIDN'T KNOW HE WAS FREE

"He hath sent me to proclaim release to the captives." LUKE 4 : 18.

EARLY one morning in the year 1831 six men were roused from their beds in the little Dorset village of Tolpuddle and told that they were under arrest. There was a father and his son, Thomas and John Standfield; two brothers, George and Joseph Loveless; James Hammett and Jim Brine. With what crime were they charged? These men were all farm-workers. Their wages were 7/- a week. They needed more, so they had joined what we call a trade union in which all pledged themselves to stand together and to ask for 10/- a week.

Their employers hated the unions and feared their power. They discovered a very clever way of attacking these men. When they had joined the union all the men had taken an oath to keep all its business secret. Now under an old law it was illegal to take such an oath of secrecy, and the men were charged with plotting. They were arrested, tried and found guilty. Their punishment was cruelly severe. They were sentenced to be sent to work as convicts for seven years in far-off Australia.

This was too much even for those hard days, and the nation was shocked. It called the men martyrs and demanded that the sentence be revoked. The Government eventually listened to this outcry and declared that the men would be pardoned and brought home. But, it took six months, in those days of sailing ships, for the news to be sent to Australia. When it reached that country the Governor out there started to argue, and it takes a long time to argue with a man who is six months away from you! It was eighteen months before that Governor gave in and the men were declared free. But even then no particular trouble was taken to find the men and tell them, because they had been sent off to lonely farms to work.

Now I want you to think in particular of what happened to James Hammett. In the first place we know now that he was an entirely innocent man. He had never joined the union or taken any oath. *But his brother had.* In order to shield his brother James allowed himself to be arrested and sentenced. This was wonderful brotherly love. In the second place, when the pardon was announced James was working on a very lonely sheep-farm. One day, *four years* after he had landed in Australia, he happened to see an old newspaper lying about, so he picked it up to pass away the time. In that old paper was an account of the pardon of these men from Tolpuddle. Then and there he realized that he was free. But for that chance he would have served all the seven years. He was a free man and did not know it!

Why do I want you to think especially of that strange situation? Because there are millions of people in the world at this moment who are free and who do not know it.

If you go to India, you will see men making great and painful pilgrimages to distant shrines, you will find men who sleep on beds of nails, you will find men who starve and cut themselves. Why? In the end you will find that there is one answer. " To get rid of the burden of their sins." They go in terror of the results of their past and long for forgiveness, to have it all wiped out.

Or go to Africa and you will still find there the witch-doctor a great power among the peoples. Why? Because simple men and women have so many fears. They fear so much in life and in death that they seek the help of spells and magic to rid them of bad luck and the evil eye and cruel spirits.

Or come and look around this country. We ministers sometimes ask people to become members of the Church and to join us at the Communion. What are we told? " I'm not good enough!" They feel they are still tied to the past, to its failures and mistakes and sins.

But Indian, African, Englishman are all wrong. Jesus came to bring to all men God's wonderful *free* forgiveness. They are free of their burdens of past sin and present fear. God forgives because God loves. To believe that wonderful message is to feel the burden drop off, to be free to love and serve.

We must reach out in this and into other lands to proclaim the good news, to see that every man hears and knows the glorious good news of the loving, forgiving, saving Father of men. In the name of Jesus we proclaim release to the captives.

17

SONGS IN THE NIGHT

" In the night his song shall be with me."

PSALM 42 : 8.

WE think of the day, with its warmth and sunshine, as the time when all the birds sing. Certainly that is the time when those we know best, blackbirds, thrushes, chaffinches and robins can be heard. But there are some birds that sing at night. The best month in which to hear them is probably April or May, when the nights grow shorter and warmer. Choose a night with a full moon and you will be surprised to find that there are birds about then.

Two of the birds that are awake and can be heard at night you will be able to name at once. There is the owl and there is the nightingale.

You can hardly speak of the owl as singing. He makes his strange call over and over again, Tuwhit, Tuwhoo! and he sweeps past on his fluffy and silent wings in search of his prey.

The nightingale is, of course, the finest of all our singers. He is a small, neat bird, very shy and rarely seen by any of us. But that glorious song of rich notes warbling and bubbling forth can never be mistaken, especially if there is a nightingale in a tree near your house and he has a mate some distance away and each sings to the other all night! I know people who have taken extraordinary pains to hear the nightingale : and I know people in whose presence it isn't safe to mention our most wonderful singer at all!

Now, which other birds might we hear on a midnight ramble? I can think of two more, the corncrake and the nightjar.

The corncrake is a shy, strange bird which does not like to fly. When he is disturbed, he runs at an amazing speed, and by night and by day he calls out, " Crake! Crake!" Again, it is not a very musical sound, scarcely to be called singing. But perhaps the corncrake is like some of us and does just the best he can.

The other I mentioned is the nightjar. That is another shy bird, with a long tail and sharp wings and a short head and beak, but a beak that can open very wide. When he flies off he opens that beak and so catches little flies and beetles and moths that are out by night. While he flies he often gives a sharp clear whistle, and when he perches he makes a low, throaty sort of noise, more like a purr than anything.

So, while we sleep in our beds at night there is quite a lot going on in wood and field, and there are songs in the night.

It is not only birds that sing at night. We read in the Psalms, " In the night his song shall be with me." Whose? God's. All the grand songs of faith will be in this man's heart and mouth during the hours of darkness.

I expect that he means that in the long, dark night he will have no fear with such songs to cheer him. The song of God's love and the song of God's care will be with him. He won't be afraid of the dark. Are you? I have known boys and girls and grown-ups who were. Perhaps they never knew or had forgotten God's song.

How could anyone be afraid if all the time he could hear,

> The King of love my shepherd is,
> Whose goodness faileth never.

God is a God of day and of night, and the writer of the Psalm knew that there could be no fear where God's song could be heard.

Then, again, I think he may have meant another sort of night, when all is sad, difficult and dark. He will still remember God's goodness then. So he will be strong to endure. He will never lose heart or lose faith. He knows that God will see him through.

Look at the story of the slaves on the cotton plantations in America. What helped them to endure? Those wonderful songs of faith which they sang together and which we call " Negro Spirituals ". In simple ways they chant in those songs of God who sets the captives free, of God who welcomes all His children in Heaven. The lifting up of their voices was also a lifting up of their hearts.

We all have times of trouble sooner or later, when work is hard, when friends seem unkind and we feel that no one cares. But God always cares. We can say with another Psalm, " The darkness hideth not from thee; but the night shineth as the day : the darkness and light are both alike to thee."

God's songs turn night to day, and wake the sad heart to sing.

18

A PRECIOUS AUTOGRAPH

" His name shall be on their foreheads."

REV. 22 : 4.

THERE was one sort of nuisance as a boy that I never was. I never collected autographs. But almost all my friends on the county cricket ground did. No sooner was play over than, book and pen in hand, they rushed for the pavilion and pestered the players to sign in their book. I understand that it is much better organized now and that you hand your book in one day and get it, or someone else's, back the next day. And I have heard that the worst thing about playing for Australia is that you are under orders to write your name so many times every day on the voyage here so that there will be enough autographs for all the admiring little boys and all the admiring big girls who want them.

But perhaps we are not being fair. Collecting autographs is quite a grown-up and respectable hobby, especially if it means securing the autographs of famous people long dead. In America, for instance, there has long been competition to collect autographs of all those who signed the Declaration of Independence when the States separated themselves from Britain. There were fifty-five men who signed the Declaration and the second man to sign had the odd name of Button Gwinnett. Let me tell you a bit about him.

Button Gwinnett was born in a little Gloucestershire village where his father was rector for over forty years. He grew up in Bristol, moved to Wolverhampton and then went to America. In America he set up as a shop-keeper. He was appointed a magistrate in 1767, and then in 1776 he was a delegate from Georgia to Congress. It was as a member of Congress that he signed the Declaration of Independence. And the very next year he fought a duel and died.

Collectors trying to make complete sets of the fifty-five signatures found that Button Gwinnett's was the hardest to get. Twenty-seven were in complete sets, and nine others were known in part sets, and that was all. So, if ever one was offered for sale, it fetched a high price. Within fifteen years that price rose like this, £520, £570, £2,800, £5,700, £10,200!

Now while he was in Wolverhampton Button Gwinnett had once or twice been chairman of a Committee at the old Blue Coat School. One day a search was being made in the old records of the school when someone found that Button Gwinnett had signed the minutes of three different meetings in 1761. Each signature was worth . . . ? Well, if one had recently sold for over £10,000, you can make a rough guess how valuable a treasure had been discovered. It was a wonderful chance for the collectors of autographs, and when they had taken it the school was much enriched.

We collect autographs here in Church. You can read about it on the last page of your Bibles (Rev. 22 : 4), " His name shall be on their foreheads." Whose name? The name of Jesus, His signature, shall be on the foreheads of His people.

What a strange idea! Strange to us, but not so strange in those far-off days when slaves were sometimes branded on cheek or temple, and when some carried marks to show what God they belonged to and worshipped. They understood what was meant when Jesus said that He would mark His people, write His name in ownership upon them. He meant that they would have no furrows of anxiety, no bumps of bad temper, no lines of suspicion. But, frank, open, pleasant, honest and kindly, their faces would bear the signature of Jesus all across them.

I read once of a traveller in India who visited a mission-school where there were Christians and non-Christians at study together. He managed to pick out correctly which were the Christians. He said it was written on their faces, a different look altogether.

I think after this talk some of us had better sneak upstairs, when we get home, and have a good look at ourselves! And, don't let us come down moaning and making excuses because of the shape of our noses or the colour of our eyes or the size of our mouths. It is what we do with these features that matters. What expression do we wear? What shines out from inside?

Men looked into the face of Jesus and saw the glorious, radiant loving face of God. Men should see written in ours the likeness of our Lord, His name, the proof that we are His.

19

SPOILING A PICTURE TO SAVE A LIFE

I WONDER if you ever make a blot? You will be writing something out, very carefully, line after line, and it begins to look a splendid piece of work and you will soon just have to go and find someone to show it to, when there is a bit of a jerk and there lies an ugly blot right in the middle. And you could cry with vexation! Or you will be painting, perhaps, a map in three or four colours, and all at once you get just a bit too much paint on your brush and all your work is wasted. Oh, I know you can get the paint off and smooth it all over, but it never looks the same.

Next time you make a blot, remember that once a man's life was saved by the making of a blot.

Come with me to St. Paul's Cathedral in London. I wish I could really take you, for it is so hard to describe what it feels like to stand inside that great Church. You feel dwarfed by its colossal size. This is especially true when you stand under the Dome and look up and up and see people walking round the Whispering Gallery, just tiny figures far away. On the inside of the Dome itself you will see that pictures are painted. Once they were lost away up there in the dark but now they are all lighted up.

Those pictures were painted by Sir James Thornhill, an artist who worked for Queen Anne and was knighted by George I. I wonder what he thought when he was commissioned to paint these vast pictures in such an extraordinary place? It must have called for a lot of careful planning. Even so, it proved so difficult and so dangerous that it nearly cost the painter his life. It was like this. One day he was working away, high on his narrow platform, with an assistant working beside him. Having just put in a careful bit of work, Sir James did a very natural thing, just what you or I would do. Forgetting where he was, he stepped back to get a better look at it! He was within an inch of crashing to the floor when his assistant saw the peril his master was in. What could he do? Call to him? No, for in turning Sir James's foot might slip. Grab him? No, for almost certainly Sir James would draw back and the two might fall. What, then, could he do? He seized a brush and cast a great blot of paint straight into the middle of the work which Sir James was admiring. And Sir James felt as we do when the blot falls. With a cry of horror and rage he leapt forward—and his life was saved! It spoiled the picture, but it saved a life.

Do you know, I sometimes think that God " spoils " things for us in order to save us? Everything is going swimmingly. We are passionately interested in sport, say, or in dancing, or in films. We get so interested that we forget other things that matter. We are losing life. It is then that God smudges the picture to save us. Perhaps we have to move house and our friendships are changed and, as we say, it isn't the same. We have to stop and look around and find some fresh interests. Sometimes there is an illness : sometimes we have to be told at home that there isn't enough money for these things. We are furious. It's a rotten " do," we say. Things are ruined. Then as we get older we see that it was a good job that they were, that the jerk pulled us up short and gave us another chance to arrange things better.

I wonder if you have ever had a thorn in your hand? It's a miserable feeling until you get it out. But suppose it is deep and you have to go to bed with it in? It does hurt and throb. Well, St. Paul had what he called "a thorn in the flesh," something always with him as hurtful and irritating as that. No one quite knows what it was. Some think it was the weakness of his eyes: others think it was fever with terrible headaches. I have sometimes wondered if it was that he couldn't sleep. Whatever it was, he asked God to take away this thing that was spoiling his life. But God didn't. The blot on the picture stayed. And what happened? St. Paul found that this trial and weakness made him hold all the tighter on to God. It didn't really spoil the picture of life: it made it richer than ever in the end. It taught Paul things that he could never have known without this trouble. Those things he has taught all the world and you and me, and one of them is surely this, "We know that to them that love God all things work together for good." Yes: even the blots on the picture.

20

A ROUSING SIGHT

At Haworth, a village away up on the Yorkshire moors, a hundred years ago, there was living a wonderful family. It consisted of a father, a son and three daughters. When you learn of the great English writers you will learn about the daughters, Charlotte and Emily and Anne Brontë. You will hear how Branwell the wild son died, how Emily died and how Anne died, and how Charlotte went on writing and caring for her father. As she grew more famous, he grew more sad and lonely; even when she was in the house he shut himself up alone in his study for hours and hours. So, when she had been to London Charlotte would try to cheer her father with tales of what she had seen. She found out that deep within him was a warlike spirit that loved to hear of arms and armour. Therefore she visited some of the great collections. Perhaps you have been to the great Armoury in the Tower of London and have seen how marvellous it is. It must have been even more marvellous to hear Charlotte Brontë describe the grim steel plates, the chain-mail, the helmets, the crossbows, the swords and daggers, the maces and battle-axes. Old Patrick Brontë would sit spell-bound. His eye would sparkle and he would be alert with interest as he pictured the weapons and their wearers.

This happened not once, but again and again. As Charlotte and her father sat before the fire in Haworth

Parsonage, with the cold wind scouring the moors outside, she reminded him of these tokens of the colourful
past, and he would be stirred to new life.

I can think of sights that should wake our spirits,
which are much nearer to us than the great national
collections of armour.

A great historian says that we should never see a town
or village without thinking that each was once a pioneer
settlement in the wilds. It began in far-off days with a
few rough dwellings in a clearing amid forest and
swamp. I find it thrilling to look at our towns and
villages to-day and to think of those who were our ancestors, the pioneers of long ago.

And I find it thrilling to look at a Church and then to
picture the pioneers who began its life. For every Church
began with a few dauntless men and women, believers,
who were certain that they must have a place in which
to meet and worship. So they worked and gave and
sacrificed, watched and prayed, and we are here to-day
only because of these pioneers. Some will see with the
eyes of imagination John Wesley and his splendid
preachers, some will see John Bunyan or the grave
Puritans, and others will go back to the first Christian
missionaries to Britain. Behind our Church-life lies a
story to thrill us all.

And I find it thrilling to take up a hymn-book. For
behind hymn after hymn is romance. Psalm and
Christian song have been wonderful weapons in the
Christian armoury. They were used by Luther, by
Cromwell, by Wesley and by Booth. On battlefields, in
dungeons, on land and sea, in sorrow, temptation and
joy men have turned to hymns until words and tunes
tell a marvellous story. Take only one example. There
is a splendid tune which we all use which is called

" Martyrdom." Why that grim name? Because it was a favourite tune of the Scottish Covenanters when they were being bitterly persecuted for their religion. They used to meet for worship out on the moors and it meant prison and death for preacher and people if they were caught. Whenever we sing that tune I can smell the heather, hear the lapwings crying, see the lookouts posted on the high rocks, and I can imagine those brave and serious people bowing their heads as a voice leads them in prayer to God.

And, above all, I find it thrilling to see the Bible and to think of what it has meant to struggling Christians. I think of those days when its pages were smuggled into this country in bales of cloth, of days when great copies were chained up in parish churches. I think of Bibles buried during persecution in Madagascar and dug up that a page or two might be passed round and then buried again. Men have risked and met death for just a few of the precious Words of Life.

Patrick Brontë had tales told to him of arms and armour. We have so much more. If our hearts grow dull and we seem to cease to care, let the sight of a church, the sound of a tune, the feel of a Bible page, wake our souls to life again.

21

AN ESSENTIAL PART OF SUNDAY

" Remember the Sabbath day, to keep it holy."
Exod. 20 : 8.

A POSTER was suddenly seen in our town. On it were five words which caught my eye:

AN ESSENTIAL PART

OF

SUNDAY

When I first saw them, I went on repeating them over and over again to myself, " An Essential Part of Sunday." I wondered whatever it meant. What was essential to Sunday?

Perhaps we had better make the meaning of that word " essential " quite clear. My dictionary says it means " indispensable." That only puts one long word in the place of another! " Essential " means what you cannot do without. An engine is an essential part of a train. The hands are an essential part of a watch. Scholars are an essential part of a school. Then, what is an essential part of Sunday? What *must* we have? What is that something without which it just isn't Sunday any more?

I began to make a list of things which some people I know do think are absolutely essential to Sunday. Here are three:

AN ESSENTIAL PART OF SUNDAY

1. *Lying in bed!* We smile, but that is quite true. Not just tired fathers and mothers but great healthy lads and girls think it isn't Sunday unless they can lie in bed in the morning. But it can't be essential, because some of us get up earlier on Sunday than on any other day. We look forward to it and jump out of bed to welcome it. A man once stayed for some weeks with members of my church. " Do you know," he said to me afterwards, " I could always tell it was Sunday as soon as I woke up. If it was Sunday, your man was up whistling and singing like a lark!" The " hearts that with rising morn arise " find the joy of Sunday in something more than having a long lie.

2. *Sunday dinner!* Is that an essential part of Sunday? Most certainly for some people! It is the day when all the family can be in, and so mother cooks as good a meal as she can. That's very nice. But " essential " does not mean something that is just nice, but something that you cannot do without. I know ministers and Sunday School teachers and all sorts of other people who have their Sunday dinner on Saturday so that there shall be less, not more, for mother to do on this day, and so that dinner shall not take too long. They want the time for other more important things. So the dinner cannot be essential.

3. *Sunday clothes!* They are something that we used to think an essential part of Sunday. The nicest and the best that we had was worn then and, often, only then. Little girls had special frocks and little boys had special suits, and grown-ups had the same. But hard times, such as a war brings, ended all that. Many had to work on Sunday then, and most had no very special clothes left to wear. So Sunday clothes went out of fashion : but it was still Sunday, even without them.

I had puzzled all that out when I chanced to ride past one of the posters again. Then all at once it dawned on me what it meant. Across the top was printed the name of a well-known Sunday newspaper! This paper was claiming to be an essential part of this day. It wasn't Sunday unless you took this paper and read it. All I can say is that some of us have never made a habit of reading a Sunday newspaper. We like to forget some things on this day and to remember others: and it is still Sunday.

No. Not one of the things we have thought of so far is really essential.

But I do know what is: the rest, the quiet, the worship. What makes Sunday different is that it is a day of rest. If more and more people go to work, if we make them go to work by the way in which we spend Sunday, then it won't be Sunday any more. Don't make a mistake about that rest. It has been given us for a purpose, so that we may all have time for God. The rest is nice. It is good for us. But great nations have lived in days past without it. It is what that rest makes possible that is essential. On this day we have time to remember the Lord our God, time to pray and praise, to think and thank and learn. Let us fix on this essential thing and our Sunday will be the happiest day of all the week.

22

A GREAT DISCOVERY

ONE of the great books which you must read in the years to come is called *The Story of an African Farm*. It was written by a woman, before it was thought women could write. So Olive Schreiner pretended that it was by a man and called herself Ralph Iron. But her secret was discovered and she became famous. This is a story of her childhood.

Olive, as a little girl, was brought up in South Africa a hundred years ago. South Africa was then a country of wonderful wild creatures, zebras, giraffes and lions, of monkeys and elephants. It was a country of wild men, Bushmen and Kaffirs. It was a country of adventure, of long, long journeys by horseback and in covered waggon. It was a land of romance and riches for some. Olive's own brother was made wealthy by finding a great diamond at Kimberley.

In this strange, exciting land this little girl began to grow and learn. There were no schools. Her mother and her brothers and sisters taught her to read. There were few books. So the book that she came to know and to love best was the Bible.

One day, when Olive was not yet eight, she was reading by herself while her mother was talking with some friends. Turning over the pages of the Bible little Olive came to St. Matthew, chapter 5, and there she began to read. You know the words :—

> Blessed are the poor in spirit : for theirs is the kingdom of heaven.
>
> Blessed are they that mourn : for they shall be comforted.
>
> Blessed are the meek : for they shall inherit the earth.

As she read on the little girl's eyes opened wider and wider. What wonderful words! What beautiful promises! What a perfectly amazing world it would be if people would listen to these words of Jesus! " Give to him that asketh " it said, and " Love your enemies." These were things that even a little girl could understand, and do. But, and this was the puzzle, even a little girl could see that people were not doing these things. Why ever not? Why, she said to herself, they can't know about them! Somehow they have all missed this chapter. How marvellously lucky that she had found it at last. She must tell them about it. At once!

So Olive caught up her Bible, and hugging it tight she ran and burst into the room where her mother was talking with friends. " Mother! Mother!" she cried, " Look what I've found!"

" My dear Olive," said her mother, " you mustn't dash in like that. It's so rude. You haven't said ' Good afternoon '."

" But Mother, listen!" And with shining eyes, and stumbling a bit over some of the words, but full of excitement, Olive read :

> Blessed are the merciful : for they shall obtain mercy.
>
> Blessed are the pure in heart : for they shall see God.
>
> Blessed are the peacemakers : for they shall be called sons of God.

She stopped, and looked up. No one seemed surprised. Polite and calm, but a bit puzzled by this funny child, they sat there.

" Mother, isn't it just marvellous?"

" Yes, dear, all our Saviour's words are marvellous."

Then suddenly it began to dawn on Olive. " But did you know them before?" she asked, bewildered.

" Of course I did," said her mother. " I learned them when I was a little girl like you. We all know them and love them. Now be a good girl and run along."

And Olive went off again with her Bible, scarcely able to believe her ears. " They knew all this all the time," she said to herself. " They weren't a bit excited. They weren't running around telling each other what beautiful news it was. They weren't doing anything about it. They had just got used to it."

It was like watching a bucket of water being poured over a fire. She felt a terrible heartache, being disappointed and utterly bewildered.

Yet Olive was right. We do get too used to the wonderful words of Jesus. We do just read them in our Bibles and hear them read in church and then forget about them every day. It is time we went back to read again with surprise and excitement the words of life, to hear what they say and to do what they tell us.

We read that when Jesus first spoke the words people were astonished : they marvelled : and they said that no one ever spoke like it before. They really did stand with wonder on their faces, holding their breath, waiting to hear whatever He would say next. What He said so struck and startled them that they never forgot a word of it.

Listen again how it begins :

Blessed are the poor in spirit : for theirs is the kingdom of heaven.

There is no need to go further than that. He did not

say, " Blessed are the great kings, or the rich merchants, or the mighty captains." He said, " Blessed are the poor in spirit "—the quiet, loving and trustful. They are the contented, the happy-hearted. They find friends. They rejoice in God's love and care. They *are* in His wonderful and everlasting Kingdom.

No. Don't go any further now. That is enough. That is wonderful and wonderfully true. To learn that and to live like that and to show others how true and wonderful it is, that would be a splendid start. We should soon go on from that.

23

NO WEEDS—NO FLOWERS

" Let both grow together until the harvest."
                                        MATT. 13 : 30.

THERE was a man once in Coventry who was worried
about weeds. Although I never actually met the
man, I know that that was his trouble. It was the weeds
in his front garden which worried him most, not that
he saw them often but because everyone who passed the
house did. His neighbours managed to keep their gardens
tidy, but weeds seemed to love his path. They flourished
in his flower-bed, and his bit of grass seemed to grow
twice as fast as anyone else's so that it always needed
cutting. At last, unable to bear it any longer, he determined to do for those weeds once and for all.

He got into touch with a contractor, asked him to
come along and see the garden and then explained what
he had in mind. The contractor was a bit staggered.
" Well, yes," he said, " I suppose I could get the stuff
and do it. But I'm not at all sure that you'll like it when
it is done. It's a bit drastic, you know."

But the worried man stuck to his guns.

And the contractor said they could come and start
next week.

Next week they came. There was a lorry and three
men, with a wheelbarrow, shovels, picks and a roller.
They tipped the lorry and out crept a black, tarry,

messy mass. Then for two days they worked. They
levelled the ground and beat and rolled it hard. Then
on top they spread the tarmac and rolled it flat. And
that was that! The passers-by, and I, saw it and marvelled. There would not be any more weeds there for
ever.

Yes, but what else? There would not be any flowers
there for ever, either!

We all like gardens without weeds. But what is a
garden without flowers? In Japan, at Kyoto, there is a
famous garden which consists of white sand and five
low groups of rock. But that is not our English idea of
a garden. We have lovely flowers with lovely names,
gillies and sweet-william, pansies, hollyhocks and love-
in-the-mist. We want flowers in a garden and for the
sake of the flowers we put up with the weeds, making
them as few as we can, but knowing that we cannot possibly get rid of them altogether.

You can see that. I wonder if you can see this? It is
a bit harder, but if you think a bit harder you will see
it. We would all like a world with only flowers—good,
kind, loving people. But can we have it? Can we have
a world without weeds—the crooked, the foolish and the
bad?

Sometimes we hear people say, " Why doesn't God
wipe out all the bad people?" Perhaps, if He did, there
could not be any good people either. No weeds, no
flowers! No sinners, no saints!

Jesus, of course, did not make it as hard as I do. He
told a story and said that God's world was like a farm
all sown with wheat. An enemy came and sowed weeds
amid the wheat. When wheat and weeds started to grow
together, the labourers said, " Shall we get to work and
pull up all those weeds?" The Master answered, " No.

You would only disturb the roots of the wheat. Leave both to grow together. We will separate them, one from the other, at harvest-time."

So it is with us, both good and bad grow side by side in us, in the Church, and in the world. God wants flowers, wants our love and help, wants to see us good and kind : but often He has our forgetfulness and meanness and idleness.

Why does not God *make* us good and kind? Would you think much of a present which a friend was *made* to give you? God wants us to offer Him the flowers of goodness with love and joy. So, leaving us free to grow them, He leaves us free to grow the ugly weeds too. If we are to be *free*, it must be free to grow both.

So that is why God bears with the weeds and lets the bad go on. It is not because He likes it : He hates it. But He knows that ground that grows weeds can, may yet, grow flowers. So, with wonderful and merciful patience, He waits and waits.

Can it be we who are keeping Him waiting for those flowers?

24

KNOWING THE WAY HOME

"The ox knoweth his owner and the ass his master's crib: but Israel doth not know, my people doth not consider." ISAIAH 1 : 3.

MAN has always marvelled at the wonderful way in which some animals can find their way home. A cat or a dog will be taken away to a new place. Then it is missing, lost. But several days later it will turn up at the old place all weary and worn. I once read a letter in a newspaper which claimed that a toad kept coming back to a garden from which it had been moved, travelling on the last occasion more than half a mile. Perhaps we all find that hard to believe. But to prove just how obstinately an animal is sure of its own home, let me tell the sad story of Dr. Oldys and his horse.

Dr. William Oldys was the vicar of Adderbury 300 years ago. It was the time of the Civil War. Now Dr. Oldys was a King's man. His people were not. So he had to leave his church and village and fly to Banbury and make a home there. Thinking that things were fairly quiet in the south of England, Dr. Oldys set out one day with his wife to take his son to Winchester where the boy was to start school.

A neighbour overheard these plans being made. He was one who hated the King and all his followers, so he sent news to the Parliament forces of the journey that

Dr. Oldys was making. And so, *not* by chance, on the way to Winchester the travellers were very scared to see troops moving ahead of them. They could not tell at that distance whose troops they were. Dr. Oldys wanted to take no risks. He was sure that his wife and son would be safer without him. So he sent them on ahead. As they drew nearer to the troops, Oldys himself watched carefully. Sure enough they signalled to him to fly, for the soldiers were Parliament men and were clearly looking for someone.

As Dr. Oldys turned his horse to fly, he was seen. Then began one of those chases so thrilling to see in a film! In a desperate attempt to delay his pursuers Dr. Oldys resorted to an old trick. He thrust his hand deep into an inner pocket and brought out handfuls of gold coins which he scattered on the highway as he raced along. He hoped that greed would be strong enough to make the soldiers forget their duty. But his pursuers kept on. They could not gain on him and it seemed as if he would reach Banbury first and thus be safe. And so it might have turned out, but for one thing. The road to Banbury lay through his old village of Adderbury. As he galloped into the village and down the main street, his horse began to slow down and outside the old vicarage he stopped altogether and would not budge. As fast as his frenzied master pulled his head round toward Banbury, so the horse angrily reared and turned back to the vicarage which he remembered so well. This was home for him.

It was only a matter of moments before the pursuing troops were there. In vain the vicar spurred and beat his stubborn steed. He turned to face his foes in despair. And then a cruel thing was done. A shot rang out and he pitched from the saddle, dead. His horse stood there and snorted and could not understand why his master did not get up and open the gate and lead him into his old stable.

More than two thousand years before the tragedy of Dr. Oldys the men of Palestine had watched their animals, the ox and the ass, and had noted their sure knowledge of home and master. And those wise old people drew a contrast between the animals with their wonderful memory and man who so easily forgets. These dumb creatures know their master and their home. Man's master is God. His home is with God. But man refuses to obey his master and he makes his home in this world without God. And then he is unhappy, feels lost, finds trouble, makes wars. All the time God is watching and waiting as the Father did for the Prodigal Son while he was in a far country. He found his way home, didn't he? And what a welcome was there, what new happiness for him and his Father! So our happiness is found as we obey God, love and serve Him and never turn away.

There is a wonderful saying which has come to us across many, many centuries. A wise man, thinking out loud to God, said, "Thou hast made us for Thyself. And our hearts are restless until they rest in Thee." God is their home. They are safe and joyful in His love. Wise and happy are we, if we know our Master and our home.

F

25

A DANGEROUS PRISONER

*" They made me keeper of the vineyards; but
mine own vineyard have I not kept."*
                              Song of Songs 1 : 6.

A King once took a General prisoner in battle. The
General turned out to be a terribly dangerous prisoner. So what did the King do? Did he have him
loaded with fetters and put in a dungeon? Did he put
him on some lonely island? Did he have him killed off
out of the way? No, none of these things. He let him go!

The King was Louis XII of France who loved to be
known as "The Father of his people". In 1509 he
fought at the battle of Agnadel and there captured the
opposing General, a man of Venice. Being noted for
his chivalrous manners, Louis XII received the General
with all the honours due to his rank, showing him the
utmost consideration and courtesy. It was a mistake:
for the General began at once to put on airs. He grew
so proud and insolent that Louis could endure it no
longer. He found himself growing more and more enraged. He called for the officer in whose charge the
General was. "Take him away," commanded the King,
" and let him go, or I shall lose control over myself and
regret it. *I have conquered him: I must conquer myself.*"

I think that that is one of the wisest things that a
king and soldier ever said. Such a one may win great

victories and rule over great countries, but unless he can rule himself and conquer his own temper, he is not worthy of his position. He is like the man in the Old Testament who confesses that they put him in charge of a number of vineyards and he couldn't even look after his own. The man who would rule men must start with the man he has most to do with and knows best, his own self.

We read in our history books of Alexander the Great. He was a great soldier, one of the greatest who has ever lived. But he was a drunkard and a man of terrible passion. In a fit of jealousy he seized a spear and stabbed his foster-brother Clitus to death. He died after a drunken orgy at the age of only thirty-three. He loved to wear a diadem and to be treated as a god, the greatest ruler on earth. But he had no control over himself, and although he was a great soldier he was certainly not a great man.

In our Bibles we read of the greatest of the Jewish kings, King David. We love that story of how he rose from being a shepherd boy to sit in the highest place of all. He ruled the largest kingdom that Palestine was ever to know. They made him keeper of the vineyards, *but his own vineyard he could not keep*. There was a fatal weakness in his character. You know that terrible story of how he had a brave soldier sent to certain death so that he might steal his wife. Because he could not control himself, David could not control his family and all the sadness of Absalom's revolt and death was really the King's own fault. A man who is weak with himself will sooner or later be weak with others. His power is only sure when it includes power over himself.

Years later there was born " in royal David's city " one who was to be the King of all men. How was Jesus fitted to rule? By growing up in that home in Nazareth, learning all that His parents could teach Him, doing what they told Him and waiting until God should call Him. Don't you think that He sometimes felt that Nazareth was a dull little place and that He was having to wait a very long time and that being a carpenter was a poor way of getting ready to proclaim God's wonderful Kingdom? But He went quietly on until He was a grown man, a man of thirty. And through it all He was learning, just as you and I learn, the hardest lesson of all and the most important, how to rule Himself. He was winning that conquest before attempting any others. It was that victory which proved Him a King of men and which brought them to follow Him in strange and dangerous paths.

Who knows which of us may not be called one day to a great responsibility? We may have to deal not with things but with people. Then, if we are to be ready, the first person we must deal firmly with is our own self. If we are in command there, then all will be well. See to your own vineyard first!

26

FORBIDDEN TO SPEAK

" Having been forbidden . . . to speak."   ACTS 16 : 6.

IT was a good man whose word I can trust who told me this. It seems that one day he was walking down a busy street when he saw, a little way ahead, an old friend, a minister. So my friend hurried after him, and catching him up, gave him a clap on the back and cried out, " Fancy seeing you! How are you?" The minister turned round with a very strange look on his face. " In fact," said the man who told me about it, " he looked for a moment as if he were going to burst." Then, he put his hand into his pocket and drew out a card and held it out without saying a word. Across the card was printed this single sentence :

I HAVE BEEN FORBIDDEN TO SPEAK.

What? Forbidden to speak! Why? By whom? By his wife? Or by his church? No. By his doctor, of course. It seems that this old minister had some serious trouble in his throat. The doctor thought that the best treatment would be to give the throat a complete rest, and so he had given this remarkable order. It looks as if the order had been very hard to obey. After all, it must have been very difficult to explain by signs that he must not talk, and why. So someone had this bright idea of having the card prepared bearing those startling words, *" I have been forbidden to speak."*

If you have any imagination, that calls up all sorts of pictures and possibilities. How very awkward at tea when you want the jam and they answer your rude pointing by passing the tomatoes, and then the salt! How marvellous for a minister to go to meetings and then just to pull this card out! Yes, and how very maddening to hear other people talking and not to be able to join in and put them right! No wonder the minister was described as looking fit to burst. To go on bottling things up day after day must have been terribly trying. Then, after doing his best to be silent for a month or more, what would it feel like when the doctor said, "All right, you can talk again"? What would be the first words he would say?

The strange thing is that all this is not so modern or rare as we might think. If we look back into the book of *Acts* we can read there how St. Paul went a long journey into Asia Minor. He went to tell the good news of God's love shown to men in Jesus. But he was forbidden to speak! Those very words are in the Bible. Paul wanted to: and yet all the time he was sure in his heart that God was saying, "No." So, puzzled, obedient and silent he went on. He thought at first that God wanted him to swing away to the north, but no, it seemed that he was to go on westwards, but not to speak. So he went on, until he found himself on the coast with nothing but the sea before him. And then, all at once, it dawned on him. When God forbids a man to speak, it is with a purpose. God did not want St. Paul to spend longer in Asia. He brought him straight to the coast so that he might cross the sea and speak of Jesus Christ in our own continent of Europe.

Are we ever forbidden to speak? Yes, on many occasions. When unkind and untrue things are said about us, we are forbidden to speak. When wrong things are being talked about and others are joining in, we are forbidden to speak. We are forbidden to speak the untrue word, the unkind word, the unbelieving word. " Thou shalt not bear false witness," says the Commandment. " Thou shalt not take the name of the Lord thy God in vain."

Isn't it a job to do as you are told and to keep quiet? We must not talk in School. But we do! We mustn't talk in Church. Well, it isn't really talk when all we do is to pass a few remarks! Yet here I am quoting the Bible to you, and saying that there are things which we are forbidden to say and times when we are forbidden to speak. And it is *such* a job to keep little tongues still! The Bible knows all about that. It knows that it is hard to keep grown-up tongues still, too. It says that men are clever enough to tame all sorts of wild creatures, but man fails to tame the tongue. Man does: but that does not mean that the tongue cannot be tamed. We belong to Jesus, who, " when he was reviled, reviled not again," who stood silent before Pilate. Jesus promised that when we have to speak for Him, He will help. It is equally certain that when we have to keep silent for Him, He will help too.

27

FIVE GRAINS OF CORN

" This day shall be unto you for a memorial, and
ye shall keep it a feast to the Lord."

EXOD. 12 : 14.

WHAT would you do if you came in to dinner on the
last Thursday in November and found five grains
of corn on your plate? I know what you would do. You
would look at them very suspiciously : then you would
look up to see if the rest of the family was laughing at
you : and then, probably, you would say, " What's the
idea? Is this meant to be a joke? If so, it's a very poor
one. Pass the potatoes, somebody."

But if you had lived in that part of America called
New England, years ago, you would have understood
at once what it meant. That last Thursday in November
is Thanksgiving Day in America. It is a great holiday,
a day for a feast when you simply have to have turkey.
It is really a sort of Harvest Festival and it goes all the
way back to 1621 when the Pilgrim Fathers celebrated
the gathering in of their first harvest in the new land.

But why five grains of corn? It used to be the custom
in New England where the Pilgrim Fathers landed to
put these five grains by every place around the table on
Thanksgiving Day. To be eaten? Not really, but to
remind all who were present that during the first terrible
winter at Plymouth, Massachusetts, the settlers were so

short of food that the ration for each was just five grains of corn. 120 men and women set out in the *Mayflower* in September 1620 and by next March nearly fifty had died. At one time there were only seven left who could get about to care for the rest who were ill. Such a terrible time called for dogged courage, and found it. So Americans remembered and still remember the suffering so heroically borne. The five grains of corn just stood for all that. The splendid spirit of the pioneers was recalled that the same spirit might live on and face the new difficulties of today.

Does that remind you of anything in the Old Testament? Of course you remember the Passover. That famous Jewish feast has been held every year in the spring for more than 3,000 years. A lamb is sacrificed and then it is roasted and eaten with bitter herbs and unleavened bread, and in haste, just as it was on the night when Moses led God's People out of Egypt. The Bible (Deut. 6 : 20) pictures a Jewish boy asking his father why they keep this curious feast and being told that thus they keep alive the memory of the sufferings and faith of their forefathers in Egypt and of the power and love of God who so gloriously delivered them from Pharaoh. Every year this feast came round, just like the American Thanksgiving Day, and as the old story was told again every year, it was never forgotten. Children learned it from their parents, and then when they grew up they passed it on to their own children. In this way, being proud and thankful for the past, the Jews were made strong and patient in every generation.

Does all that remind you of nothing in the New Testament? I see a table in an Upper Room in Jerusalem at which there are gathered thirteen men, twelve and One Other. During the meal He takes bread and breaking it He hands a portion to each, saying, " Take eat . . ." Then He takes the wine cup and passes it to each, saying, " Drink ye all of this . . ." And then He says to them, " Do this in remembrance of Me." And in remembrance of the Lord Jesus this is done in some churches every day, in others week by week or month by month. A Table is laid with bread and wine and round it gather the disciples of Jesus to take the bread and the wine as He commanded. Why? What for? That tiny portion of bread, those few drops of wine, are nothing in themselves. Like the five grains of corn and the lamb and bitter herbs, what matters is what they stand for. They are, as we say, *a symbol*. The bread which is broken and the wine which is poured stand for Jesus whose body was broken and whose blood was shed on the Cross in love for men. In that way they are like the corn and the lamb. They stand for so much. But in another way they are different. We believe that as we take the symbols of Jesus, Jesus Himself truly comes to us. We receive His bread and His wine that we may receive Him. So we call the bread and the wine not just symbols but *a sacrament*. They are outward things which God has set apart that He may give with them a special blessing. Just as soon as we understand and believe that, Jesus wants to see us at His Table that the special blessing may be ours.

28

WHOSE PICTURE GOES IN FRONT?

" I live; yet not I, but Christ liveth in me."
GAL. 2 : 20.

IF I asked you to name the most famous detective who has ever lived, I have a strong suspicion that quite a few would answer, " Sherlock Holmes ". Then the rest of us would laugh in a rather superior way because, of course, he never lived. Sherlock Holmes was a character invented by a writer called Conan Doyle. Now Conan Doyle wrote many books that are still first-class reading, such as *Micah Clarke, The Lost World*, and *The Adventures of Brigadier Gerard*. But one of his books into which Conan Doyle put most was *The Great Boer War*. He had served in the war as a doctor and he knew the courage and strength of the men on both sides. The book had to be printed again and again until at last it was brought out as one handy volume of 500 pages. This was eagerly awaited, and when it was printed and bound the publishers, Messrs. Nelson and Son, sent a copy to the author. And he sent it straight back and demanded that every single copy of the new edition be altered!

Why? There weren't any printing errors. The pages were in the right order. The cover was strong and a fine colour. What was wrong? The picture which every reader saw on opening the book! There, right at the front, the publishers had put a picture of—the author.

Conan Doyle was furious when he saw it, not because it was a bad picture, but because it was the wrong picture. He said that the picture to go in front of a history of the Boer War was not the picture of the man who wrote about it but the picture of the General who won it. So he demanded that his own picture be taken out and that of Lord Roberts be put in its place. Conan Doyle was big enough to put himself in the background. Glory must go where glory was due.

Now we'll go a journey to see an example of a very different spirit. The journey is to Oxford, to see the very oldest College of all, Merton College, which will soon be 700 years old. One of the oldest parts of it is the Chapel, in the windows of which there is some very precious stained glass. In the Choir there are fourteen windows presented by Henricus de Mamesfeld in 1300. Who was he? What was he like? Look at the windows and you will see. You cannot very well miss it. In each of the fourteen windows are three figures. In twelve of them there is one apostle and two pictures of Henry himself. So he managed to get twenty-four pictures of himself into fourteen windows! Someone has called it, " One of the most astonishing examples of vanity that has come down to us from the Middle Ages ".

How men differ! There was a man who must have his picture to the fore. Conan Doyle insisted on putting the other man's picture first.

Let us go a bit further afield than Oxford and back further than the Middle Ages. We go back to the New Testament times. A missionary is in Corinth when he gets very bad news of the churches in Asia Minor. He writes to them a long earnest letter. To help them he tells what had happened to him. He had grown up one kind of a man, a man he learned to pity, even despise.

That first man was dead; and yet, says Paul with a smile, " *I* still live." Suddenly, there, he breaks off and realizes that he is putting himself forward too much. He changes the full-stop to a semi-colon and writes, " I live; *yet no longer I, but Christ liveth in me.*"

Paul wanted those men and women and boys and girls of Galatia to forget him if only they would still remember the Lord Jesus, to love and serve Him until He became all their life. It was Jesus' picture which filled Paul's eyes and which he held up before the eyes of others all his life long.

> Yea, through life, death, through sorrow and through sinning
> He shall suffice me, for He hath sufficed:
> Christ is the end, for Christ was the beginning,
> Christ the beginning, for the end is Christ.

29

DON'T FORGET THEIR NAMES

"There is a lad here . . ." JOHN 6 : 9.

Y̲ou have never heard of a boy called George Brewster, have you? Yet, once, all England rang with
his name. He was a boy of fourteen who lived at Cambridge. He was a chimney-sweep, working for a brute of
a master. One day George and his master went out of
Cambridge to sweep some chimneys in a house in the
country and his master made George climb up the chimneys, yes, inside, to scrape the soot down. This had
been forbidden by law in 1840. It still went on, and so
in 1863 Charles Kingsley wrote his book *The Water
Babies* to tell people that it still went on. In 1864 another
law was passed. But it still went on, so that in 1875 this
cruel forcing of boys up filthy, narrow, stifling chimneys
had not been stopped. Our George came out of his chimney alive, but only just, and in two days he was dead.
Then the good Lord Shaftesbury returned to his fight
for these lads. He told the story of George Brewster until
people were shocked. That very same year another law
was passed which really put an end to chimney sweeping
by boys for ever. It was 75 years ago : but it would not
be right to forget George Brewster's name. To remember that and to think of him somehow makes it all so
much more real.

Now I don't suppose that you have ever heard of

DON'T FORGET THEIR NAMES

James Greenlees, have you? Yet, ten years before Lord Shaftesbury had everyone thinking of George Brewster, every doctor who was alive and awake was hearing of James Greenlees. Who was he? He was just a boy who was brought into hospital with a very badly broken leg. His leg was examined by one of the wisest and kindest doctors in the world, the great Joseph Lister. As he looked at this crushed and broken thigh, Lister was asking himself, " Shall I? Dare I? If I don't, he is certain to lose his leg, almost certain to die. If I do, it *may* help the leg to heal." Do what? Use something to kill the germs which were getting into the wound. Lister had just learned about germs and he believed that carbolic acid would kill them. The year was 1865, and so far no antiseptic, as we call these things, had ever been tried in this country to keep a wound clean and to help it to heal. As Lister stood by James Greenlees' bed he made up his mind to take the risk. So, this boy of eleven was the one on whom the power of carbolic as an antiseptic was proved. It was the beginning of a long fight against germs in which untold suffering has been prevented and in which millions of lives have been saved. But, again, it all becomes so much more real if you remember the name of the boy with the broken leg by whose bed Lister made his great decision.

It is so easy to forget names, or not even to trouble to learn them. " Oh, some boy," we say. " Some girl." That means we have never really looked at them or loved them.

I have always wished that the disciples had been more careful about this. You remember that before the Feeding of the Five Thousand a lad was found with five barley loaves and two fishes. " There is a lad here," said Andrew to Jesus, all grown-up and careless-like. The boy had a name hadn't he? Why not use it? I am sure that Jesus said, "A lad? What lad? Bring him to me." And when the boy came what would Jesus' first question be? "Hello, son," he would say, "what's your name?" Perhaps it was Joseph. "Well, now, Joseph," Jesus would say, "that's a large lunch you've got there for such a small man. Could you spare it for me? I won't eat it all myself!" And young Joseph would look up at Jesus with a bit of doubt in his eye. He would be wondering if they were making fun of him. He didn't much like letting his lunch go, but Jesus looked at him so fair and square that he felt it was all right. Jesus took the loaves and the fishes and the multitude was fed. And, I'm sure that Jesus saw the boy afterwards and said a great "Thank you" to him. He was more than just "a lad" to Jesus.

People mattered to Jesus. He did not push by, too busy to look at them or to learn their names. He stopped to hear about their pains and troubles, and He remembered. He says that God knows us and all about us, where we live, our names, our needs. "Why," said Jesus (and I'm sure that He said it with a smile), "God knows how many hairs there are on your head!" I shouldn't be surprised if some of the wise old teachers, who hadn't much hair left, didn't put up their hands to their head and give a chuckle at that. They knew what Jesus meant, that each person and all about him matters to God, just as each one matters in a family. And each has a name as a sign that he really matters.

Once there were some special enquiries being made in a big city and a man had to go from house to house asking, among other things, how many children there were. He knocked on one door which was opened by a large, homely woman. The man explained who he was, and then he said, " Now, Madam, what children have you?"

" Let me see," said the woman, "there's Billy and John and Fred and Sam, and then the twins Sally and Susie . . ."

" Here," broke in the man impatiently, " it's not names but numbers I want."

" Look here, mister," replied the woman, " we haven't got to giving them numbers yet !"

If there were twenty in a family, every one would have a name. In God's great family every one has a name. He knows your name and mine. He is our Good Shepherd, and the Bible tells us " He calleth His own sheep by name ". How careful we should be if God knows us so well, how confident. We should be confident that we are never forgotten : we should be careful that our name is one which it gives Him joy to remember.

30

STEALING FROM GOD

" Will a man rob God?" MAL. 3 : 8.

A KING in a rage could be very dangerous indeed in olden days. Officers spoke in whispers and courtiers kept out of the way. He might throw a spear as Saul did at David, or like the Queen in *Alice in Wonderland* he might go stamping about and shouting, " Off with his head!" He would most surely find someone on whom to spend his anger.

But suppose he was in a rage with God? What in the world could he do then? How, and it is so terrible a thing that I hardly like to ask it, how could he spend his anger on God?

One of our English kings can tell us. Eight hundred years ago there came to the throne of England one of the very greatest of our rulers, Henry II. He came to the throne when everything in the country was upside down. He found his kingdom in a terrible turmoil. People were suffering bitterly from the quarrelling and fighting of the nobles. After reigning for thirty-five years Henry left the country quiet and orderly under a strong government. This he managed to do, although he had a huge kingdom to govern. We call him Henry II of England, but his rule extended from Scotland to Spain. He was King of England, Duke of Normandy and Count of Anjou. Thus he was a great monarch in the eyes of the world. But what sort of *man* was he? He could be wise, just and strong : he could also be weak, cruel and altogether foolish. The root of his weakness was his temper, a temper which broke out against man—and God.

If I say to you, " Thomas à Becket ", you will remember at once his anger against man. Thomas à Becket was the Archbishop of Canterbury. He had been a close friend of the king but that did not mean that as Archbishop he would agree with all the king's wishes. On one special matter he stood firm against the king, utterly refusing to obey. Henry, who was in Normandy, hearing of a fresh act of defiance, cried out in fury that his subjects had no spirit or they would not thus allow him to be made a laughing-stock. They would rid him of this traitor. Four knights heard the cry. They planned together, crossed to England and found the Archbishop in his Cathedral before the very altar. There they killed him, a deliberate and cruel murder which came from the king's anger.

Eighteen years later, in the last year of his life, the king was driven from the French town of Le Mans as it went up in flames. Again, he was boiling with helpless rage. He turned to look at the town and wild words escaped him, wicked words which he spat out against God.

" For that Thou, O God, hast taken away from me this day the city that I most loved in this world, wherein I was born and bred and my father lieth buried, therefore I shall requite Thee. For from this day forward I shall take from Thee the thing that should please Thee most in me, *and that is my heart*."

" Will a man rob God?" asks one of the Old Testament prophets. He thought of men keeping back their gifts from God's house and God's worship, and many do rob God in that way. But this is a far worse theft, for a man to rob God of the love and devotion that should be His, to steal away his own heart from God. Henry was right. A man's heart is what God wants most.

Let us forget the unhappy king robbing God and think of the joy we can have and the joy we can give to God by bringing to Him these hearts of ours in love and faithfulness.

> What can I give Him,
>   Poor as I am?
> If I were a shepherd
>   I would bring a lamb;
> If I were a wise man
>   I would do my part;
> Yet what I can, I give Him—
>   Give my heart.

31

CAPTURED BY PIRATES

PATRICK was a farmer's son, and they lived near the mouth of a great river, the River Severn. In that lay their peril. One day there came creeping up the river with the tide a fleet of pirate craft. Their goal was the rich farmsteads of Britain and their richest booty was men. These they carried off in hundreds to sell in Ireland as slaves.

It all happened in the distant dark ages fifteen hundred years ago, but people felt the same then as they do now, and to Patrick, a youth of sixteen, it was a ghastly thing to be carried off, and offered for sale in return for cattle. He was then a slave. His head was shaved. He was dressed in a rough sheepskin. He was, he said, " humbled every day in hunger and nakedness." His principal job was to herd swine, and like the Prodigal Son before him he was ready to make their food his.

Yet other food was given him, food for his soul. In those long years of bitter hardship he found the friendship of God. Alone, Patrick found he was not alone. There was One to whom he could tell it all and from whom his help would come. In those days of prayer and servitude Patrick vowed himself to God's service. But any prospect that this desperate young slave would be able to keep his vow did not seem great.

First he had to find his freedom. But how? He dwelt with a cruel heathen from whom he could expect no mercy. To escape was well-nigh impossible, and if he did, how could he cross from Ireland to Britain? The impossible was done. Patrick escaped. After six years, when the youth of sixteen had grown up into the man of twenty-two, he slipped off, journeyed two hundred miles through unknown country and reached a port. There was a ship about to sail, but the captain would not take Patrick on board. The sailors insisted that he should. Where was the ship going? Patrick did not even know that. He was sure that God was leading him home. Thus began a journey whose details we would love to have. For three days they sailed. To Scotland? Then they landed and pushed for twenty-eight days through wild country. Down into England? On they went for another fourteen days before they came to a large settlement. There Patrick ran away from his new masters. So at length he found his way back to his relatives in Britain, a free man.

Patrick had now to decide how he would fulfil his promise to give all his life to God's service. He made up his mind to become a priest. How could he do this who had been a slave so long, who had seen no books since he was fifteen? He could do it with God's help. With tremendous persistence Patrick set himself to study in France, first in this monastery and then in that, until he knew his Bible, at least, as no other man did.

It was just then that he had clear and startling dreams. He seemed to see a messenger arriving with letters, one of which was for Patrick. Across it was written " The Voice of the Irish ". Even as he opened it he seemed to hear many voices crying out, " We beseech thee to come and walk once more amongst us ". So it was that Ireland called him once more to return as her missionary.

But his teachers and masters did not agree at all. They said that Patrick was not the man for such a task, not clever enough. It was altogether too great a risk to send a missionary to heathen Ireland in any case. However, Patrick kept on talking about the call to Ireland until I believe that they were all glad to see him go. In the year 432 he was made a bishop and set out for the land of his sufferings which had become the land of his dreams.

At that time Ireland was a country of many tribes, each with its own king, all heathen. There were only a few small, weak groups of Christians. His work was to strengthen the Christians and to challenge and persuade the heathen. Immediately he landed he brought himself to a king's notice by lighting a forbidden fire on a mountain at Easter-time. The old record says he kindled it " in the nostrils of the king ", which was nearly as bad as Sir Francis Drake singeing the King of Spain's beard! Sure enough Patrick had to appear before the king, and that gave him all the chance he wanted of telling who he was and what was his mission and what was his message.

How tirelessly he worked in the coming years, going from tribe to tribe, winning king and people, baptizing them, building them churches and training for them ministers. We are shown a picture of him by an old writer, " not deterred by cold . . . sleeping on a bare stone, with a wet cloak around him, a rock for his pillow . . ." In ten years he had the Christian church in Ireland growing so wonderfully that Christians everywhere were talking of a miracle.

But some people will hurt even men who can work miracles. Patrick had a friend, a close friend to whom he had told some of the secrets of his life. And one of the secrets was about some wrong he had done as a boy.

Once when Patrick's work was being discussed, this friend, possibly in jealousy, repeated what Patrick had told him and said that he should be called back from his work. And he was. For a moment Patrick was tempted to give it all up. But he fought the temptation, challenged the decision and in the end was allowed to go back to end his days in the work he had begun and which had been so blessed.

Saint Patrick was not an Irishman, but Ireland calls him her saint. He loved the land and brought it into God's fold. I agree with a writer who says that the greatest sermon Patrick ever preached—and by the way, he once preached for three days and nights so he was something of a preacher!—I say that I agree with the writer who declares that the greatest sermon ever preached by this great preacher was *his own life*. He obeyed that New Testament command, " Let us not love in word, neither with the tongue; but in deed and truth."

32

COPYING A COPY

" Copy me as I copy Christ." I Cor. 11 : 1
(Moffatt).

FROM time to time gold coins are found in Britain.
Sometimes they are turned up by the plough : sometimes a tree blows down and they are found at its roots.
Often they are not very good gold, nor are they very
beautiful coins. Go to any good museum and you can see
some of them. Perhaps on the slip underneath you read
that they were made for King Cassivellaunus when
Julius Caesar came to Britain, or by King Tasciovanus
his grandson. Is all that on the coins? No. The king's
head was not put on coins as it is to-day, often there was
no writing, and sometimes there were just a few letters.
It all has to be puzzled out by clever men. And
" puzzled" is the word. Because, apart from being old
and worn, the coins were poorly made. These early
British coins were copies of coins made in France. The
French coins were themselves copies of coins made in
Greece some hundreds of years before.

Now if you look at one of the gold Greek coins, you
will see how splendid it is. On the heads side is a picture
of the god Apollo with fine long wavy hair bound by
a laurel wreath. Turn to the tails side and you find a
picture of a chariot drawn by two bounding horses.

Look at the first copy, that made in France. Frankly,

it is a mess. The man who made the coins was beaten by that head and the hair and the laurel wreath. It came out on the coin as a collection of blobs ("pellets, tassels, hooks, bosses and strange crescent-like forms," one book says!). And if he could not do a head, the maker was even more beaten by the tail. Two horses were quite beyond him, so he tried one. A good one? Listen to the book. It says it is a horse "that is strangely distorted and runs some risk of falling to pieces". The chariot, by the way, *has* fallen to pieces. "Mere dots and streaks," the book says. So much for the French coin.

What about the British which was a copy of this copy? The British coin-maker obviously looked at the patterns on the French coins, first one way and then another, and then gave it up. The heads side, which you remember was all pellets and tassels and hooks and bosses, did not suggest a head at all. The Briton thought it was a pattern which had slipped. So he took the bits and arranged them neatly round a space where he learned to put a few letters of the King's name. When it came to the tail, the Briton did better. He did know a horse and chariot when he saw one. He put new life into the horse that was falling to pieces, pulled him together so to speak. Yet, with all our pride in our own country we cannot say of these old British coins that they are very beautiful. They are copies of very poor copies and no more.

Something is always lost in a copy. So a copy of a copy is getting further and further away from the original.

We are called to copy Jesus Christ, to live like Him and to imitate Him in all our ways. Do we? Is it Jesus Christ that we copy or Father, Mother and all sorts of other people? And whom did they copy? Do you see?

COPYING A COPY

If we are only copies of copies we shall be getting further and further away from the likeness of Jesus. Of course, we learn from Father and Mother to begin with. Just as new Christians learn from their missionary. But soon that missionary has to say what Paul said, " Copy me *as I copy Christ*." His people were to look back to the original. Where Paul was an exact copy of Jesus, they could follow him safely : but wherever he was a poor copy, they were to go straight to Jesus and to copy Him. So we are to copy Father and Mother, and the minister and our teachers and anyone else, just so far as they faithfully copy Jesus *and no further*. If we are to be like Him, we must all the time be going back to Him. And we find this, if we look back into the long story of our churches. Whenever men have turned again to Jesus, when they have read about Him carefully and lovingly, when they have made Him their Friend and Guide and Pattern, then new life has come back into those churches.

We want every fresh lot of boys and girls that comes along to mean the words they often sing,

> May we copy closely
>   Him we so much love,
> Till we bear His likeness,
>   Perfected above.

33

CAMELS AND HORSES

"He that endureth to the end, the same shall be saved." MARK 13 : 13.

WHAT is the difference between a camel and a horse? If you have a pair of eyes, you might say, or even a nose, you will soon find that out.

We all know that a camel is tall and rough and has a hump (or is it two humps?). The camel's feet are large and soft. He is a real grumbler and he can be very savage. The camel kneels down to be mounted and he can go days and nights without a drink. He is the carrier of the East, the ship of the desert, and his back can be broken by the last straw.

Of course we know more about horses. We know how massive a shire horse can be and how tiny a Shetland pony can be. We know that a racehorse is sleek and shiny and walks as if he had springs in his heels. Stories are told of how intelligent and how faithful horses can be. The horse is the steed of war, and we could tell of famous horses and their names.

But all this has not answered the question, " What is the difference between a camel and a horse?" I found that question and its answer in a book about Australia. It was about a special part of Australia, the Red Centre, as it is called, some of the hardest and hottest and most barren country in the world. In exploring it both the horse and the camel were used, and the great difference between the two was made plain. This is what the book said, " Adversity, which mirrors a camel to the best advantage, tends to show up all that is worst in horses."

Give a camel a hard time and he comes out strong : give a horse a hard time and " most horses show signs of throwing up the sponge long before their chances of pulling through are gone." Camels doggedly plod on : horses just pack up.

Are you a horse or a camel? We all fit into one group or the other. We join the horses and give up easily, or we join the camels and keep going on.

We like to think of the English as the nation which goes on. When Captain Scott and his companions were on that fearful journey back from the South Pole, Captain Oates's frostbitten feet were in a terrible condition. He began to slow up the speed of the march, and the lives of all depended on speed. He turned to his friend Dr. Edward Wilson one day and cried out, " What shall I do? What *can* I do?" " Slog on, old man," said Wilson, " slog on!"

I like to think that the people of Jesus Christ are the sort who slog on. He spoke with hope of those who would " endure to the end ", which just means keeping on keeping on and never, never giving in. If that is hard, the Christian has a promise. " I will be with him in trouble," God says. We are never left to struggle on alone. That was the great comfort of David Livingstone in the wilds of Africa. However lonely he felt amid savage men and places, he had what he called the word of a gentleman, " Lo, I am with you alway, even unto the end of the world." So, he plodded on.

Or I think of our great Oliver Cromwell in that bitter Civil War. He had set his hand to the plough to win freedom from the oppression of King or Bishop. It was a long, hard struggle and more than once it looked as if the Parliament Cause would be lost. It was Cromwell who stood firm, Cromwell with the burning faith. One of his fellow soldiers wrote of him, " In the dark perils of war, in the high places of the field, hope shone in him like a pillar of fire, when it had gone out in all the others." It was to Cromwell that victory was owed.

It might give your friends a bit of a shock to be told that you were a Christian and a camel. They might even say rudely, " A camel? Yes, I always knew you had a hump!" But now you know what I mean by bringing both together like that. To have splendid dreams is not enough. You must also have the patience and grit to work them out. We would learn to live and do splendidly for Jesus Christ. That is our dream. Then let us set ourselves to turn dream into fact. It calls for camel-qualities that of us men may say,

> There's no discouragement
> Shall make him once relent
> His first avowed intent
>   To be a pilgrim.

34

CHRISTMAS IN NEW ZEALAND

"Behold I bring you good tidings of great joy, which shall be to all people." LUKE 2 : 10.

I FIND it hard to imagine what Christmas feels like on the other side of the world. We have always known Christmas in the winter. As we get into December we begin to ask ourselves, " Will it be a white Christmas this year?" Everything looks so different with this soft mantle of snow cast over it. Everything sounds so different, so much quieter. It is all real Christmassy, as we say. And people have felt like that in England for hundreds of years, ever since the first Christmas celebrated in England, which is so long ago that no one can say when it was.

How very different it must be to go out to Australia or New Zealand. There Christmas comes in the middle of the summer. In place of our winter there is blazing sunshine and in place of football there is cricket. Parties must seem all wrong and certainly plum pudding must seem all wrong. Fancy having to look for a cool corner of the house in which to pull crackers! Even more strange it must be to sing the carols when everything is so different. Instead of hundreds and hundreds of years of customs going further back than men can remember, a land like New Zealand can tell you when its very first Christmas was celebrated. It was on December 25, 1814.

That was the first time is was Christmas in New Zealand.

We must go back a bit in the story, to 1793. In that year a young minister called Samuel Marsden went out to Australia. It was only six years since the first load of convicts had been shipped from Great Britain to that distant land. Everything was rough and ready and life was hard. But Samuel Marsden was not afraid of a hard life. He set to work to arrange schools for the children, homes for orphans and a mission to the blackfellows. Among the dark-skinned natives he was struck by some who were different. He met them in New South Wales and found them to be finer, stronger and more intelligent. He learned that they came from New Zealand and were called Maoris. Soon after his first meeting with the Maoris, Samuel Marsden came back to England. There he spoke of the people of New Zealand and of his longing to get into touch with them.

When Samuel Marsden got back to Australia and spoke of his determination to reach the people of New Zealand with the message of Jesus Christ, people laughed at him for a dreamer. Why, there wasn't a sea-captain anywhere who would dare make the voyage. The Maoris were famous fighters and to attempt to land was to go to one's death.

But Samuel Marsden was not the man to be put off by hair-raising tales of clubs and cannibals. At last, and not until 1814, he managed to find a captain who undertook to take him and his party and to land them in the North Island. And, very wonderfully, it was Christmas Day when they went ashore in the Bay of Islands. Samuel Marsden was first, and in the presence of suspicious and dangerous natives he conducted a Christmas Day Service. He spoke from these words, " Behold, I bring you good tidings of great joy, which shall be to all people." Then, I imagine, he told them of the One who came as a little baby, weak and helpless, to be the very Love of God among men, to bring peace and joy to all.

It was this mission begun by Marsden which won the friendship of, and made peace with, the natives and made it possible for white men to enter that beautiful, rich land. So began a long, long story, the story of modern New Zealand, in some parts sad, in some parts thrilling, a story not yet finished. The most thrilling part of it is the story of the Maoris and the white man and how they have learned to live together. Once a terrible war broke out, but peace was made again. At one time it looked as if the natives would die out under the white man's rule, but that will not happen now. They are growing in numbers and sharing in government.

So when Christians celebrate Christmas in New Zealand they can rejoice that the peace and goodwill which Samuel Marsden preached 140 years ago have both come to stay. Never mind the things which make our Christmas and which they lack. They have the real thing, joy in the gift of Jesus Christ who brings love and peace among His people. If we have that, wherever we are and however we celebrate, it will be a real and a happy Christmas.

H

35

I DO WISH I HAD SEEN HIM

WILLIAM Hazlitt was a brilliant English writer who died 120 years ago murmuring, " Well, I've had a happy life." Probably one of the finest things he ever wrote is an essay, half a dozen pages, *Of Persons One Would Wish To Have Seen*. Why, the very title starts you thinking. Of all the wonderful people of the past, whom do we wish we had seen? Hazlitt says he talked about it with a group of friends, and being writers it was natural that they suggested the names of several great writers of the past. But almost at once they realized how much a writer can differ from his writing. You read an exciting book of adventure, all about swords, ships and sharks, and the writer is the meekest of men. Or you read some beautiful lines of poetry and when you see the poet you find he is both hefty and hearty. So some one wisely suggested that it is not great *names* that are wanted but great *persons* : and the two do not always go together.

The friends with whom Hazlitt talked it over could only suggest one statesman whom they wished to see. That's very strange when you think of it. When a statesman is in power, everyone knows his name : but how soon he is forgotten! Who was it that they wanted to see? Oliver Cromwell, " with his fine, frank, rough, pimply face, and wily policy ". Some people speak as though he was a most wicked villain and others as though he was a saint. Perhaps if we had seen him we should know what he was. It is so much easier to understand people, if you have met them.

At this point the friends began to discuss the great actors of the past, much as to-day we might discuss film-stars. When they get into the middle of that someone suddenly says that all the names mentioned so far have been men. Aren't there any women of the past anyone might wish to see? Honestly, there weren't many! Most great women of the past did their work quietly behind the scenes. Those who didn't might not be the best company, Queen Elizabeth, for instance!

One of the friends said he had just thought of two strange characters whom he would have liked to meet, Guy Fawkes and Judas Iscariot, especially Judas. " I would fain see the face of him who having dipped his hand in the same dish with the Son of Man, could afterwards betray Him." Thinking of Judas made them all pause and fall quiet, until someone said, " There is only one other person I can think of after this . . . If Shakespeare was to come into the room we should all rise up to meet him : but if that person was to come into it, we should all fall down and try to kiss the hem of his garment."

We all know who it was that they meant. But were they right? If Jesus came into the room, should we kneel to Him? Or, what should we do? Would we be delighted or rather afraid? We sing about the people who gathered round Jesus " I should like to have been with them then ". Are you sure? We ought to know, *because we do meet with Him.*

He has promised that where two or three of His people gather, He will be there with them. We believe that He is here with us now. There is no need to talk of people one would wish to have seen. We do meet Him. When we come into His House we often hear the words, " Seek ye the Lord while He may be found, call ye upon Him while He is near ". He is indeed near, to help and to bless every one. We " draw near with confidence " because we know that He comes near to us in a love that casts out all our fear.

36

A HAPPY WARRIOR

THE highest decoration that any Englishman can win is given " For Valour ". It is awarded for valour in the face of the enemy, this coveted Victoria Cross. Books have been written about the wonderful feats that have earned the decoration and we thrill to read them. But there is one thing we should remember. Courage in the face of the enemy is not only shown by soldiers, nor is it always known at the time.

Let me tell you of a famous man whose courage has thrilled me. You know him as a writer, Sir Walter Scott. When you hear his name, you think of *Rob Roy, Ivanhoe, Kenilworth* and *A Legend of Montrose*. People who know a little bit about his life say, " Sir Walter Scott? He must have been the most famous writer that ever was, popular and wealthy and a friend of George IV. Wasn't he the man who built himself a great mansion and was Laird of Abbotsford?" All that is true, but there is a grand story behind it.

When he was only a child, Walter had an illness that left him lame all his life. For one who grew up to love the out-of-doors and who longed to be a soldier, that was something to be faced and overcome. The very fact that he grew up such a sensible, cheerful man shows his courage in the face of that enemy.

That Walter Scott was one of the hardest working men who has ever lived is proved by a shelf-ful of his books. Six years after the first 'Waverley' appeared he was knighted and became Sir Walter. He was now famous and rich, when all at once he was taken with a terrible and mysterious illness. Once his doctors thought he was dying. For thirty months he was grievously ill. Yet in those thirty months Sir Walter Scott wrote five of his most famous books. That was a masterpiece of courage. But, even more wonderful still, in those five books there is not a single trace of the writer's misery. He kept it to himself and just wrote on. The five books, by the way, were *Rob Roy, The Heart of Midlothian, A Legend of Montrose, Bride of Lammermoor* and *Ivanhoe*.

The poet Wordsworth wrote a noble poem on *The Happy Warrior*. He says that the happy warrior is one

> Who doomed to go in company with pain,
> And fear and bloodshed, miserable train!
> Turns his necessity to glorious gain.

Sir Walter was doomed to pain in those months, and what an astonishing harvest he reaped. His printer, James Ballantyne, tells us that when the printed volumes of the *Bride of Lammermoor* were put into the author's hands, Sir Walter read them most anxiously, for " he did not recollect one incident, character or conversation." He had dictated the book while in such suffering that it had blotted from his memory all he had written. Pain is one of the enemies from which we all run! Here was courage in the face of the enemy indeed.

That courage was to be needed when Sir Walter Scott had recovered from his illness. Seven years later he faced a worse trouble. The firm of printers with which he was associated had run up great debts which they could not pay. Sir Walter felt himself responsible for paying back the tremendous sum of £130,000. There was an enemy for a man of 55 to face, to have to slave away year in and year out to earn money to pay off debts for which he was not entirely responsible. How did he face the enemy? With all his old courage. In the very week in which this terrible blow fell, Sir Walter Scott wrote a chapter of his book *Woodstock* each day. In that fearful time he just settled in more steadily to his job and was as kindly, patient and steadfast as ever. Before he died he had paid off all that was owing.

I have given this talk the title of " A Happy Warrior." We have seen that Sir Walter Scott was a brave fighter. What about his happiness? That he was a happy man no one who knew him doubted. I believe I have found the secret of his happiness in a sentence which he once spoke to his daughter : " Nothing really worth having or caring about in this world is uncommon." He loved all the ordinary things and ordinary people of the world. He was a man whose heart was greatly valiant and wondrously contented, a truly happy warrior.

37

HE KNOWS

"I sat where they sat." EZEK 3 : 15.

ONE of the most famous of all Russian writers, indeed of all writers, was called Dostoievsky. He was born in 1821, in old Russia of the Church and the Court and the Army. There were the Czar and his brilliant nobles. There were huge estates, boundless forests, snow and sleighs and wolves. And there were millions of serfs, pitiful slaves, whose lives were counted of little value. Wealth and misery grew side by side.

Dostoievsky was the son of a military surgeon and he knew the life of the prosperous : but he had a heart of sympathy which went out to the poor and suffering. He wrote about them in boundless pity. One day he was declaring his faith in the people of Russia and of all they would one day do when they were free. A young doctor listened to him and then said sneeringly, " Who gave you the right to speak thus in the name of the Russian people?" Without a word, Dostoievsky raised his leg and bared his ankle. There, plain to see was a ring of roughened, toughened skin. " This," he said, " gave me the right."

What was that ridge around each ankle? It was the mark left by *chains*. When he was a young man of twenty-seven Dostoievsky had been suspected of joining in a plot against the Czar. He was arrested, tried and sentenced to death. He was actually led out with others to die. Then the sentence was changed and they were sent as convicts to Siberia. For four terrible years Dostoievsky wore those chains day and night. He toiled in the awful cold, half-starved, filthy, exhausted, herded at night with criminals and other convicts like an animal in a pen. It was through this experience that Dostoievsky came to know people in a new way, as they really were, both the worst and the best in them. He suffered with them, and all the time his wonderful brain was storing up his impressions, incidents and conversations. So, when later he spoke of the people of Russia, he was not just airing ideas or using his imagination. He was drawing on real knowledge which he had gained at terrible cost. Those marks around each ankle were a kind of certificate which entitled him to speak.

Have you ever wondered how God can know all about us? He knows so much because He made us: but how can God know what it feels like to be tired or ill, to be a child, or starving, or a slave? God is the Almighty, perfect Spirit. How can He *know,* feel as we feel? If I see you fall down and hurt yourself and cry, I know what it feels like because I have done it myself. The scars are there on my knees now! If your father dies and you feel the emptiness in your home and in your heart, it is only someone who has lost a father or mother who knows exactly what it feels like. We say that God knows, but how can He?

I know how, and I can tell you. God knows *through Jesus Christ.* Jesus who was the very Love of God, came and lived as a man. You know all the wonderful story of how He was born in a poor stable and how His life was threatened by Herod at once. You know how He grew up in a home with brothers and sisters. He played and learned and grew just as we do. He had times when He was happy and unhappy, and when He was puzzled. He lost His father and had to work. He was tempted. He went hungry and thirsty and tired. He knew sadness of heart. He wept. His friends were disappointing. His enemies were cruel. He died a horrible death upon the Cross.

Living as a man, He knew it all from the inside. After He was risen, we believe that God knew it all in a new way, all about our life. The Bible tells us that our prayers are heard by One who understands perfectly. What a help it is to tell " it " to someone who understands! What is the proof? What right has Jesus to speak for us and to us? Well, He too has scars. Those scars in hand and side are the sure proof that He knows the very worst. He has shared it, and He can sympathize with us in our troubles and our needs.

I remember an old hymn which went like this:

> Can we find a friend so faithful,
>   Who will all our sorrows share?
> Jesus knows our every weakness,
>   Take it to the Lord in prayer.

Yes, He knows, and, therefore, to Him we can always come.

38

FLOOD MARKS

I WAS born in a city with a grand Cathedral, a noble river and a beautiful County Cricket Ground, all near together, the City of Worcester. For six years I went to school under the shadow of that Cathedral alongside that river; and in the summer, when morning school was over, we would stand on a high bank while one boy who was the proud possessor of a pocket telescope would try and read the score-board on the cricket-ground a thousand yards away, across the river. Now, to get to the river we went down a short slope, then down some steps and under a broad gateway, and there we were just by the Cathedral Ferry. Close at hand stood a massive, high sandstone wall, and cut into that wall were lines and dates, each one showing the height and the year of some notable flood of the past.

There are more than a dozen of these flood-marks in all, because Severn floods are frequent. The river rises away in Wales, and when there is a season with much rain the river receives from the hills more water than it can possibly pass on. Then it begins to rise, filling up its deep banks and in the end overflowing until the wide Severn Valley is a vast lake. And this record has been kept through the years of the varying heights to which the swollen river has risen.

When I saw those marks when I went to that school first in 1921, the four topmost dates were all old,

November 1770, May 1886, February and November 1852. I used to look at them and think that life had become dull: there weren't any more floods worth speaking about. 1770 and 1886 and 1852 would remain the winners for all time.

But, you know, I was wrong. In my third year at that school, in 1924, the river began to rise in June, of all months. It rained and rained that June and the river went on rising until we used to go and watch it, thick and brown, rushing past bearing haycocks it had swept from the fields, fencing poles and whole tree-trunks. So another mark was added. Since then five more have been added too. So, of the nine highest which you see to-day, six have been added since I first saw the wall! The 1947 mark is less than an inch lower than the highest flood ever recorded. Now, if you said to me, " We shall never beat that highest mark," I shouldn't believe you. It might be beaten this winter, or this summer even!

There are other high marks that, as a boy, I thought could never be beaten. I used to hear of the wonderful days of our country's past. I used to read of Hereward the Wake, of Henry V, of Drake, of Cromwell, and of Nelson, and I used to think that all the great days and all the great men lay in the past. Then one evening I listened to a voice calling to the nation to make *that* its finest hour. And no finer hour than the summer of 1940 and no finer men than the pilots of our fighters in the Battle of Britain have ever been.

Then, too, I used to read and be told of the great days of God in the past. They were there, recorded in the Bible, and I used to think that He never did anything so amazing in our day. I used to hear about the great missionaries and think that there simply wasn't anyone to-day like Carey and Morrison, Judson, John Williams and Livingstone.

But now I've come to see that that is all wrong. God has His heroes still. We have had Grenfell and Schweitzer on the mission field, a man like Kagawa in Japan. Men have died as bravely and truly for their faith in our day in Russia, China, Germany and the South Seas as ever they did of old. God's work has gone forward there during war and under persecution. He has blessed His people and built up His kingdom. When Morrison, for example, had worked in China 1807-1834 he said that it would be a miracle if in a hundred years' time there were 1,000 Christians in China. That hundred years has gone. How many Christians are there in China? Between four and five *millions*.

Before Jesus left His friends He told them that they would see and do greater things than had ever happened while He was with them. His promise has come true. So His friends to-day do not look into old records of the past to find the best that God can do. They look forward eagerly, certain that the best is yet to be.